Protocols of the Fifth Dimension

Aurelia Louise Jones

Mount Shasta Light Publishing

TELOS - Volume 3
Protocols of the Fifth Dimension

ISBN 978-0-9700902-7-0

First English Publication - April 2006
Second Printing - April 2008
Third Printing - January 2010

Mount Shasta Light Publishing
PO Box 1509
Mount Shasta CA 96067-1509 – USA

Phone: 530-926-4599
Fax: 530-926-4159

E-mail: aurelia@mslpublishing.com
Web Site: www.mslpublishing.com
Also: www.lemurianconnection.com

Cover Photography: Erich Ziller
Cover Design: Aaron Rose
Page Layout and Formatting: Aaron Rose

We, the Masters of Light, are giving you, through the simple teachings in this book, all the keys you will ever need to attain your Ascension with Ease, Grace and Wonderment.

It is now up to you to decide what you will do with this material. Will you read it once or twice, and then say, "This is interesting" and perhaps share it with a few friends, but neglect to truly integrate this wondrous wisdom into your daily life to become, in this now moment, your divinity incarnate? Or will you take this information into your Heart, studying profoundly and with full commitment the simple magical keys that will evolve your consciousness to a fifth dimensional being? Will you do it until you see us face-to-face and until you are invited to the Hall of Ascension?

It is up to you, beloved children of our hearts; you now have all the keys! As you unlock those simple but precious Keys of Wisdom within the heart, we are waiting for you on the other side, to receive you in the arms of Love!

- Adama, Ahnahmar and the Lemurian Goddess

Table of Contents

Part One
Practices and Protocols to Develop
a Fifth Dimensional Consciousness

Part Two
Various Channelings

Dedication

With deep love and honoring, I dedicate this work to God, the Creator Supreme of All, and to the Earth, the Planetary Goddess, to assist in my own way the vast expansion of Light that needs to take place for the evolution of humanity into a fifth dimensional consciousness.

I also dedicate this book to my spiritual family in Telos, to Adama, Ahnahmar, to my daughter Eliah and my son Variel, my two children in Telos who are still there, holding the flame of Love from the time of Lemuria. I also dedicate this book to the spiritual hierarchy of this planet, and to Lord Maitreya, the planetary Christ.

I invite all of you reading this material to take this seriously into your heart and allow the profound changes needed in each one of us in order to attain the consciousness of the fifth dimension and incarnate the fullness of our divinity right here on Earth. Just imagine what it will be like when all of us walk the Earth in the full power of our Divine Essence and the limitlessness of the ascended masters!

Acknowledgements

I wish to express my deep gratitude to all my friends around the world who have supported the emergence of the Lemurian Mission and to those who have published this important work in the language of their country.

I want especially to express my deepest gratitude to all the members of the Telos World Wide Foundation in Montreal who have worked tirelessly to create the structures needed in preparation for the huge expansion in human consciousness that is expected to take place around the year 2008 and beyond. I thank especially Line Ouellet who has volunteered her time many hours a week, for the last five years, to assure the success and the continuation of the mission of the Telos Foundation.

I also want to thank Gaston Tempelmann, president of Telos France, whose dedicated work supports and prepares the expansion of the Lemurian Mission in France and in Europe.

Without all of you, the miracles of Love now manifesting through the reconnection with our Telosian family and the preparation for their emergence among us could not take place. To all of you, I express my deepest gratitude and eternal friendship.

ℙreface

𝒜hnahmar and 𝒜dama

In the Love and Light of our Creator I greet you today. I am Ahnahmar, beloved of Aurelia and a member of the Council of Elders in Telos. Beside me stands Adama, High Priest of Telos and the guiding force of our mission to reunite all with the energies of Lemuria. It is my voice that you hear now as I wish for all to recognize the frequency of divine union that I share with my Aurelia.

Adama and I offer infinite blessings to all those whose eyes rest upon these pages, and all with whom their energy will be shared. Our joy today is with our beloved Aurelia as we witness her own journey of evolution and discovery. All wisdom she uncovers for herself, she recycles in her own heart, and then presents it to the world. For this we honor her greatly.

Together, our energies create a trinity of expression for we are aspects of the same soul. We have all resided within the heart of Mount Shasta for many lifetimes. Our souls are linked together in a mission of Light to extend to all on our great Earth Mother the teachings, and most importantly, the vibration of the Heart of Lemuria. Adama and I do so from one side of the veil, and Aurelia does it from the other.

Her example is one that each of you may recognize in your own hearts. Over the years, she has heard the heartbreak and cries of humanity, and has reached out to offer support and wisdom. All of you are now at the gateway of your own reaching out, and with great love and compassion, we offer our wisdom and support to you.

Aurelia's path in this lifetime is the same as yours. She strives to embody, within the transiting physicality of the third to fifth dimensional vibration, the truths of love and brotherhood that she knows in her heart of hearts. Her truths are also our truths and your truths as well, for we are all One.

With great gentleness, we recognize the intensity of emotion that exists in your dimension. The wisdom we share within this volume is the simple truth, the life truths we live each and every day in our dimension. Our souls are united with yours in the Ascension of the Earth and all kingdoms that reside upon and within Her. We hold you tenderly in our arms to soften your pathway through this journey and to bring into balance all that stands in the way of this great shift.

We ask that you share with our Aurelia the truth and the love of your hearts as she travels the planet doing the work of Lemuria. She is a unique and joyous soul whose dedication is a shining mirror to all of us. Call us to you whenever the need or desire arises. We are only a breath away. With much love and gratitude!

(Channeled by Beth Iris, incarnated in Telos as Celestia, sister of Adama)

Introduction and Welcome from Adama

It is with great love and much support from the many realms of Light of Telos and beyond, that the third volume of the Telos series is presented to you at this time of great Earth changes. I am sure you have already noticed that changes have already begun for the cleansing and transformation of your planet into Her glorious destiny. Allow this purification of the Earth, as it is most necessary for the "Mother" to renew Her body that has been so desecrated.

The material presented here is designed to stretch your heart and mind to a new level of Christhood and mastery. If you are choosing to align yourself with Earth's destiny and evolve your consciousness for life in a world of pure Love and Light, it is imperative that you create the awakening of your true divinity and make it the most important goal of your life. You must gain the full understanding of what it means to become an ascended being and the state of consciousness and the responsibility that come with it. You have played the separation and karmic game far too long. Too many of you still hold much illusion about the level of consciousness you must embrace and attain to fulfill your heart's longings for the sublime alchemy of the soul that Ascension brings.

You have to prepare the Garden of your Heart to become conscious, responsible galactic citizens to mingle, as equals, with your brothers and sisters from the Stars. You have to weed out of this garden all that is less than divine Love, perfected and transformed, by diligently and with great constancy, awakening your true nature as a divine being. You will have to reconnect in complete "Oneness and Surrender" with your Source, the Creator of All, the Heart of pure Love and Light. This is what will free you, beloved ones. All those of us who have channeled material for our third volume have already attained this level of Love, and it is with great compassion and humility that we attempt to show you how you can attain this for yourselves. It is not so difficult once you let go of your erroneous ways of living.

Our beloved Aurelia could not channel this material until she was able to understand, in the Garden of her own Heart, the level of Love and Surrender required to enter into the world of "Oneness." She agreed to reveal in this book some of the dialogues she has had with us, about her own difficulties and frustrations for your benefit and to show you that what one can attain, everyone else can also attain.

Basically, although your problems and difficulties manifest in various ways, they stem from the same core issues. The divinity in each one of you, not yet fully awakened, represents a cell of pure Love from the Heart of the Creator. You have never been disconnected. We are very grateful to our channel for the efforts she has invested into weeding the Garden of her own Heart and Soul, and writing about it, in order to assist you along your own pathway towards the "Sun of your Divinity."

This third volume presents several helpful tools, such as meditations and activations in etheric temples. You will find protocols and codes of ethics that you must embrace in order to be admitted into the great "Hall of Ascension." This book offers you the next few steps you need to be allowed to join us consciously. And it offers so much more!

Know, beloved ones, that as you read our material, we are there with you assisting your process. Our hearts long as much as yours to be together again, in the glory of the Brotherhood of Light. We are pressing on you now to come all the way "home" to the Heart of Love, through the total surrender to your unique pathway and the Will of the Holy Father/Mother, All That Is.

Let me finish this introduction with a quote from the Heart of the Creator.

"As you become again Christed beings, all you will experience is the most tender Love. I ask you to go into your heart and feel how much I love you personally, as well as every human being. Everyone is so precious, so beautiful, so amazing and unique! My heart seeks only to show you this, and to give you the Love that is your heritage. Surrender into Love, children of my Heart! That is Christ consciousness. For what is Christ? It is my living Love! And what are you! Love's vehicle!

"The truth of Love that I am is a web of Life so strong and so full, so perfect in its holographic nature, that everything is making love with everything else. This is where I am taking you, back to the gate of the eternal 'Now.' It is only when your mind is One and your heart is fully open seeing only Light that you will be 'Home.' Your thoughts and your love are the two ingredients of change riding upon the energy of your Will. Allow my Will to be fully manifested in you, and your homecoming will be accomplished in a joyous and tender way.

"The 'Attitude of Gratitude' will speed you on your way with so much Grace! Be blessed, my beloved children. I am calling you back 'home' to my Heart, where never again will you know sorrow or lack of any kind, and you will be blessed without measure. I will lay at your feet all the Treasures of Heaven! This is my Will for you. These are the gifts that I am longing to bestow upon all of you."

Adama
High Priest of Telos

Part One

Practices and Protocols to Develop
a Fifth Dimensional Consciousness

The heart that beats in your body
Is the same as the Heart of Lemuria.
Listen to it and treasure it.
You are not incomplete and
You are not incapable
Of becoming this Heart
With your entire being,
And of vibrating this frequency
Throughout your entire beingness.
- Adama

Chapter One

Awakening to a Fifth Dimensional Consciousness

Adama and the Council of Elders of Telos

Many blessings to all of you reading this material. I am Adama, High Priest of Telos.

I greet you again from my heart, and ask you to join us in consciousness for a gathering with the Council of Elders of Telos. It is in this way that the knowledge gathered from our experience, and the frequency of the wisdom gained by all of our souls, is passed along to the greater society in our Lemurian culture. We gather like this on a regular basis to conduct classes, although we prefer to call them "sharings." Each such meeting takes 4–6 hours of your time. An intention is set at the beginning that the energy shared will be transmitted to all in our community.

We gather as brothers and sisters, as mentors and students, and in this manner, share with each other the depths of our individual essence. Through this sharing, we further the evolution and expansion of our group consciousness in unity and love.

We wish to speak to you today of the protocols of the fifth dimensional vibration that you now wish to understand in order to access it for yourselves in your daily reality. The question has been asked, *"What do we need to do to ascend to the fifth dimension?"* Understand that there are preparations and purifications of consciousness that must take place. Basically, in the new reality that is now being established on the surface of your planet, the fifth dimension is not a place you will go to, but rather a state of beingness you will attain that will gradually establish the fifth dimension in your present realm.

The fifth dimension is a vibration, or rather a marriage of vibrations, represented by the energies of love, trust, compassion, faith, grace and gratitude, a frequency of the purest form.

The structures and organization of our societies in the fifth dimension flow organically from an integration of these energies by the individuals who reside here. Our Lemurian community in Telos mirrors our fifth dimensional experience as an outpouring of our combined manifestation and embodiment of these qualities in heartfelt communion with all that surrounds us.

We did not emerge from the womb with this mastery and awareness present in our consciousness, and neither do you. Even the new generations of children who arrive each day in your transitioning dimension are not fully in their mastery, although they are more awake than you were when you came. It is through the joy and the journey of this experience of Earth that we evolve.

It is through the grace of this planet that evolution is and has been a part of the experience of every soul who has incarnated here. The grace of your present time is that now you may fully awaken to your mastery, and retain this consciousness for the remainder of your soul's evolution, whether you choose to ascend and remain in this incarnation or continue to experience cycles of incarnations here or elsewhere.

We wish to share with you practices that have been the core of our spiritual evolution. We follow these practices to this day, and we share them with our children. They exist as a foundation for our constantly expanding journey through and to Creator Source. They are founded on the principle that we are all responsible for our own energy. Before unity consciousness of the fifth dimension can be fully integrated globally, this work must be done on an individual basis by each one of you. Each person must walk their own unique journey to the end; no one else can do this for you.

Most important of these practices is the offering of compassion and non-violent communication in thoughts, words, deeds and feelings. Indeed, self-compassion forms the cornerstone of the spiritual awakening necessary if one is to recognize and integrate this fifth dimensional vibration. This vibration already exists around you at all times. As the frequency of the planet herself becomes more and more refined, each one of us is responsible to purify and refine their own vibration no matter what dimension we reside in.

We do this for the evolution of our Divine Essence, and we do this for the greatest good of all kingdoms which reside on and within this glorious planet we call "Mother." This is a solemn and divine responsibility that does not rest lightly on your shoulders, and yet, confers on you a grace that is unparalleled in the history of the Earth.

You now can walk as masters and mentors yourself, even if your human form may not seem to mesh well with your remembrances of other times and places where limitlessness and infinite possibility abounded. We say to you with all of the truth that our hearts can share, that now, this present moment in Earth history, is a time of infinite possibility. This is the magical time of creation from the highest divine source to the densest in your physical reality. We know and feel your hearts greet ours in this truth, although your minds still struggle to grasp the full scope of what we are telling you. Your minds still demand ritual and rules, and proof that is irrefutable, before you will step one foot upon this new path. So we will work today with practices that, if you will allow them, can bring you back to the frequency of faith and trust instead of doubt and denial.

Many masters have shared these truths throughout the eons of evolution this planet has already experienced. But it is your experience in this lifetime that is most important. Today, you have an opportunity to hear these words again with more evolved ears, and to recognize them on a deeper heart level than ever before in your physical dimension. You have an opportunity to work with the support of all creation to bring these truths into physical manifestation. In truth, this is why you are here, and why you have been given the opportunity to incarnate at this time.

*As your respected Native Elders have told you,
"You are the ones you have been waiting for."*

We will begin with exercises that may already be familiar to you. If you have experienced them in the past, we say now is the time to experience them again with a fresh perspective. If they are already a part of your daily practices, we also say that it is important for you to do them with a higher level of understanding that will bring the true results you desire to attain. The work to be done now in your dimension is in fact quite simple; the subtleties you will witness, however, are enormous. Within each level of vibration that you access and integrate, *"the activity becomes simpler,"* but the results become greatly more expanded.

We will explore practices that awaken us all to the divinity we are meant to express, and dismantle the illusions that veil the original mind and freeze the heart. We will restore methods that will accelerate the re-awakening of your consciousness and that lead to inner freedom and an understanding of the true power of love. Level one of this practice involves the evolution of the Self.

Step One is to learn to question yourself as to who you are and what you believe from a higher perspective, not from the insecurity of the ego or the lower mind.

You must instead ask the questions that spring from the deepest pools of your heart, and then ask from the entirety of your real self, your GodSelf. Then, you must be willing to listen with the part of you that is awakened enough now to hear the answer. Do not wait for a time in the near or distant future when you feel you have reached a certain stage of enlightenment. Do not wait for a later more evolved version of yourself, whom you feel may be better equipped to receive the answer.

You are ready now, and the part of you that is open to the answer in this moment must be given the opportunity to hear it. Only if the question is serious and heart-felt will the answer be received. If the question is not asked with true spiritual intention, the universe and your own higher self will deem it mental curiosity or ego fantasy.

As you ask the question, step back into your true self, and let go of all you "think" you know about yourself. This practice is about the infinite possibilities that are present in "not knowing." You are in truth both physical manifestation and soul essence, and yet you have largely forgotten your Source. In self-questioning, you confront both essence and manifestation and begin to understand and to witness the sacred contradiction this represents.

Only when you embrace this contradiction will you arrive at the first stage of awakening your mastery.

Mastery is not about metaphysical abilities and phenomena. This first level of mastery is the experience within your own heart of being present, in the same breath, with your divine essence and the ways in which you manifest it. It is the recognition in each and every moment that your divinity is present within you, even in physical manifestation guiding your destiny in the most loving and appropriate manner.

Until you are able to hold enough compassion for yourself and live from the awareness that you hold both spirit and its manifestation within yourself, you do not allow the energy that is vital to create your mastery to permeate the depth of your soul. To become a master is to remember your true self, and yet to do so in the temple of your physical manifestation in this time and space. Ascension is nothing more than awakening to the truth of your divine self within this dimension or any other, within this body or any other.

Without self-compassion, how can one accept all of the seeming contradictions stemming from the illusion of your world? Without self-compassion, how can one hold both the essence of what one is and the outward manifestation that limits and confines that essence within the same heart and the same space of unlimited love?

It is the allowing of self-compassion that moves you into the vibration of grace. It is the fusion of the physical Earth with the etheric realms and the merging of an awakened truth with the power of love that moves you into your mastery. A master is one who recognizes the truth and grace that is present all around him, in the physical and the non-physical.

A master is one who understands within his heart, from a frequency of love and gratitude, that duality exists only between being awake and continuing to live an illusion.

When we speak of qualities such as love, trust, faith, compassion, grace and gratitude, we do not speak about mere intellectual concepts. Compassion is not an idea whose time has come. Compassion is an energy that creates great oscillations in the fabric of your universe. Grace is not a religious notion or promise, it is a palpable energy that can be witnessed and utilized in the world around you. Faith and trust are not promises made or bargains to be kept. They are the frequencies that power each breath that you take in the physical.

With each in-breath and out-breath your soul takes in the divine. Gratitude is not attained by speaking the polite statements you are taught as children. It is an energetic acknowledgment to the universe that you are in alignment with Source. And love is not a romantic or religious exclamation. Love is quite profoundly the energy that powers all of creation.

For most of you, it will take an on-going commitment to truly recognize and embrace these frequencies. It will take a daily, conscious choice to remain awake and honor yourself and all creation by living in the integrity of these energies. This is the responsibility for self we speak of. You have spent thousands of lifetimes practicing myriad ways of being. You have performed rituals and initiations as rites of passage to higher realms of being. Now we say to you that the rites and rituals, the rules and mystery schools, the codes and secrets are completely gone. The answers you seek reside within you. The only spiritual practice needed now is one that awakens you to this truth.

In Telos and all Lemurian communities of this dimension, we all affirm daily our choice to be awake and in communion with Source. It is this choice that manifests our paradise. Our world is as we create it, instant by instant.

Step Two is the recognition and dismantling of belief in all that you "think you know" to this point. This next step is indeed a leap of faith.

Please know in your hearts that we are here, holding out our hands to you when you take this leap. We cannot do it for you, nor give you a technique that will suit each and every one of you. We can, however, guide you so that the leap seems less staggering and the fear less overwhelming. We hold in our hearts all of the compassion that you will need, until you can hold it for yourselves.

We cannot teach you how to be compassionate with yourself, but we can show you how to "want" to be compassionate with yourself. For this "want" is in itself the one true question that all in the universe offers support to answer. This "want" or desire is itself a force, a tool of mastery and a tool of the awakened human being. This "want" is the voice of a human heart that recognizes, after many a dark night of the soul, that it can question, in a loving way, everything that it has always known.

This "want" is not compelled by a need, and it is not a desire for something that is missing. It is instead a knowing in the heart that everything is already here, and you must simply give it form. It is the compassion to allow all the other possibilities of creation the human mind has not yet awakened to.

We stand on the other side of that deep rushing stream which represents all that you "think you know" about yourselves, calling to you from our hearts with a sweet song, a sweet frequency. We offer our love to help awaken in you the energy to leap over those churning waters without a thought. And we will be there to catch you on the other side as you land on the shore of "unknowing."

The universe will herald your arrival with the trumpets of angels. All is appropriate in this "wanting" and "not knowing," and all is aligned with the ultimate grace that is the Divine Plan, and for the highest good of all.

It is impossible for any of you to experience this great truth and not become it. But first you must be willing to do the work to strip away the accumulated layers of illusion that hide who "you think you are" from the real you. In so doing, you will become more human, hosting a spirit living inside a body. If you embrace this truth in your heart, in compassion for all that being in a body entails, you infuse your consciousness with the light that is all of you.

This experience of ascension in a physical body is new to most of you, as it was new to most of us. This is the grace that the planet offers in this time and space. It is the opportunity to become innocent again, and to approach life, not from prior experience or knowledge, but from faith. Build the faith that this meshing of spirit makes any manifestation possible. Develop the faith in yourself that you are a master who is capable of co-creating with the universe all that is possible.

In childhood, the soul undergoes phases of change. From birth you begin to learn that you are in a place of limitation, confusion and separation from your heart and from your soul. You learn to relate through your mind, and in a specific timeframe. Initially, life is an experience of isolation until you recognize the All that is the Source of you and the universe. Your real self is timeless and unlimited.

Mastery does not mean "knowing" everything as some of you may believe. Life is a continuous process of unfolding. The Creator exists in a perpetual state of creation and so do you. True mastery is understanding how to use that which is within as well as that which is outside yourself. True mastery involves "knowing" in the moment only that which is appropriate for that moment.

Step Three is a sacred one. It is the experience of communion with your soul as a doorway to your GodSelf.

Your soul contains every emotion ever experienced by you, and relates to all experience in the now moment. As you begin to deconstruct the belief systems that keep you asleep and in illusion, do not approach this practice lightly or impatiently.

Make a list of the belief systems that limit you. These may be beliefs that others hold about you, or uncomfortable beliefs you hold about yourself. These may be beliefs that you hold about the world around you or your spiritual journey. Make a list of your "good" or "bad" beliefs without any judgment and dig deep within for the subtle belief systems, uncovering the layers one by one.

Be ruthlessly, yet compassionately honest, as nothing is hidden in the vibration of the fifth dimension. Carry the list with you and add to it, until you feel completion.

It may be difficult to look at beliefs you have so carefully wrapped around yourself for protection. Yet each of these beliefs holds a piece of your energy, a portion of your godforce that is needed for your complete awakening. And so, the moment is now, to begin reclaiming the truth of who you are, not intellectually but energetically.

Again, self-compassion is greatly needed here, if you are to surrender unconditionally to each belief system and its embedded emotions long enough to garner the wisdom and healing from it.

Before you detach permanently from the belief, you must reclaim your energy from it, or part of you will continue to be in separation.

Your soul is indeed the doorway to the awakening of your true self, for it operates both in the consciousness of separation and that of the Divine. It allows for the wholeness of self and holds all that you deem positive and negative in perception and experience. And it does so with neutrality and unconditional compassion.

Your soul holds the experience and the emotion of all the choices you have made in this lifetime and every other incarnation of your evolution. It holds the understanding of the choice you made at the time each belief system was imprinted in the ego. The ego does not create patterns of belief from malice or judgment, but through the eons of separation, it has taken over the role of protector. The ego has been the guardian of individuation for a planet and a human race that chose this experience. But now the time of unity consciousness is at hand. You are called forth to heal all that holds you back.

We suggest that you make another list of what you know, in the depths of your heart, to be true about yourself. Be equally as non-judgmental. Explore the difference between what you think you already know in your mind and the true knowingness that comes from oneness with your divine essence. To create this list you must once again delve beneath the layers of limitation, and move aside old teachings and paradigms of being. You must listen with the simplest and purest of motives.

This list will not come in words from the mind as did the first one, but from the heart as vibration. This vibration will grow stronger and clearer until you experience a tone of such unmistakable truth that you will feel the totality of your being expand. Only then may you add an item to the list because only then will you truly "know."

Add to this list from this time onward; it will continue to evolve as you awaken. The energy waves this list creates will travel through all time and space and dimensions that comprise your soul evolution. Most importantly, this list will carry your true energy. You will begin to live it in such integrity that no one in all of creation will dispute its truth. It will become a blessed tool for your mastery.

Your negative ego experiences of negativity will come to the surface with this practice. What is negativity but a perfect reflection of limited belief? What is negativity but a judgment that the ego has made to protect itself? So again, self-compassion must become your loving companion who asks in a gentle voice, "Is this the real truth of who I am?"

This compassionate voice will help you create a third list of judgments you still hold about yourself. This next level of awakening holds the opportunity for much healing. Allow your open and innocent soul to guide you now. The third list is not meant to be a burden. It is through grace that the knowingness gained here allows the experience of oneness with self to be available instantaneously. Giving yourself this gift in truth and love can be an ecstatic experience.

The transformation and freedom manifested when judgments are healed can bring a great acceleration to your journey of awakening and become a gift like no other. Have patience with yourself and with all that is unresolved in your heart. You will come to love this healing process. You will see these feelings about yourself as mirrors of the judgments you apply to your outer world. Work within the framework of compassion and allow the transmission of grace to envelope you. Allow then the transformation of judgment to unfold.

How can you embody the purity of love in a physical way if you hold yourself in judgment of anything? How can you hold the sacred vision of your true self that is the seed of all creation, if you judge? Even if you judge the judgment, you move out of the vibration that is your truth. Even if the judgment is one that you view as positive, it still carries an energy that limits your experience. Without judgment you will soon find within yourself the light you wish the entire Universe to shine with.

In Telos, we do not "know" all with our minds, but we allow each experience to be witnessed by the heart from a fresh perspective, without judgment or expectation. We feel the truth of each experience as it unfolds from a deeper place, as we stretch out to touch the energy that is all around us. We are also in transition just as you are, and we are evolving just as you are, as is the planet.

We have embodied the energy of trust through lifetimes of practice so that our experience of the energies of Source are continually deepening. We have learned through patient and compassionate work with ourselves and our children that an ever-growing understanding and awareness can be gained. We do not limit ourselves through the beliefs of the ego, and therefore, we are surrounded by the love and the infinity of Source at all times.

In our evolution, we have learned much about the heart center and how it functions in physicality. We have learned much about the true functioning of the lower mind, and how to work with it, not for it. We have learned in practical terms that *the mind is a house of questions, and the heart is a library of answers.* We have learned to love our questions and to cherish the answers the heart provides with each question.

We have learned through much practice to view all from a perspective of compassion and trust, for these are the true energies that empower us. We have learned through the practice of non-judgment to embrace all the energies of self, and to love and stay conscious of doubt and fear when they arise. We have learned that honesty is synonymous with non-judgment and that honesty must begin with self. We have learned that the greatest source of wisdom resides within our hearts. We have integrated and become this learning because of our continual practice of it.

We practice these truths each day in our conscious interactions with everyone we come in contact with. If we find ourselves expressing, in thought or deed, an attitude or

15

belief system rather than the true knowledge of our hearts, we immediately explore the opposite action or thought.

The master brings to his path all lifetimes and soul experiences. At the level of evolution on which you and the planet now find yourselves, this encapsulation of experience and the wisdom you gain from it happens instantly. All of your lifetimes are attached to this present one, and you affect them all through these practices. All that is taking place in your life and the world around you, even what you consider illusion, is a gift for your evolving awareness.

You are the ultimate mirror for your dimension. Just as we made a conscious choice to bring forth the complete mirror of ascension in our realm, in our societies and ourselves, you must now join, in a responsible way, with the ascension of your planet. You must want to awaken now to the divine love and truth that you are. You must want to remove any obstacles or limitations of self that hinder you from bringing forth this truth in physical manifestation at this time. You must want, in the depths of your heart, to be part of the human mirror you are creating, for on levels beyond your comprehension, you represent the greatest collective understanding of the God-Force that the physical Earth plane has ever known.

You are preparing your hearts as sacred ground where multitudes will soon walk. You must first receive your own homecoming, however, before you can show others the way to theirs. You must first awaken to your own truth and step back through the layers of self-judgment and separation. Claim now the parts of yourself that have been locked away from the pure vibration of love and trust.

Every evolutionary choice on this planet has to do with Self. The mind cannot comprehend these changes, but the heart can. Who you are and who you recognize yourself to be will change exponentially with a grace and power that is unprecedented when you recognize these truths. These new perspectives will then light up the strands of your DNA that have been dormant, waiting for this time. Every strand of the human DNA is designed to evolve the physical body very rapidly based on shifts in consciousness. This is why the transmissions of energy to this planet are intensifying daily. Your immune systems and your organs are learning to refute any vibration or consciousness that does not recognize the truth of who you are.

You are able in this moment, just as we are, to create yourselves disease-free, as long as your consciousness is aligned with this freedom. You are able in this moment to interact with multiple dimensions that are the matrix of your universe as long as you are awake to your own energy matrix. We speak to all of you now who are struggling with levels of fatigue that seem at odds with this truth.

This fatigue is not born of the body, although the body will learn to mirror it if experienced long enough. This fatigue is a depletion of source energy that arises from a lack of alignment with self. Living your daily existence outside the frequencies of love, trust, compassion, gratitude and grace is exhausting you.

Choosing a daily spiritual practice which dissolves the limiting beliefs and judgments that preclude you from these divine energies will restore your vital physical energy. This choice will re-align your system as if connecting the pipes of your kitchen sink, so that the energy you want can easily flow again.

Step Four of this practice is three-fold.

Each morning, upon rising, take some time in solitude to contemplate your state of being, honestly and without judgment. Ask your guides and support teams, such as us, and your own higher self, to release old beliefs and limitations that no longer serve you. Ask the universe to provide you with a new perspective each morning, and allow yourself to be in a state of unknowing with the mind and knowing with the heart.

Ask the universe to provide you with easy and graceful mirrors where needed to fully awaken your consciousness. And ask that, throughout the day, your physical energy grow in equal proportion to the conscious work you do in relation to healing yourself.

Throughout the day, work regularly with the energies of love, trust, faith, compassion, grace and gratitude. Call into yourself, into your physical body, into your cells and your DNA, the purest vibrations of these energies. You are building an energy signature in your body. You are overwriting, in effect, the old frequencies and beliefs that have limited you, with the full potential of who you truly are.

Be aware, as you go through your day, of the vibration generated by each thought, word or deed. Learn to recognize that which expands your energy and that which collapses it.

Each evening, recognize and embrace in profound honor all that you have given yourself that day. Recognize that in this giving to self you have indeed given to all of Creation. Then state the intention that while you sleep, you will continue to integrate through the heart all the new wisdom recognized that day. Ask that the cells of your physical heart and the strands of your physical DNA expand to your new vibration, and that this evolution take place for all time and space and dimensions.

In this way you will replace old patterns and imprints that no longer represent the truth of who you are. Who you are will change daily, and your new frequency, in communion with all those around you, will be felt throughout this universe and all others, back to the Great Central Sun and the Creator energy itself. With compassion, we solicit your recognition that the use of these practices does not entail forcing yourself into another consciousness. Practice means allowing yourself to open to the limitless potential that already exists within you.

These exercises are not meant to be done sequentially but simultaneously. After you have given one day of practice to each individually, practice them all together throughout the ongoing days. Show appreciation to yourself for the work you have already accomplished and cherish your awakening truth as it embraces the true you and the new world that surrounds you.

In our next gathering we will share the second level of awakening that we engender in Telos. The human heart holds much more love than it can ever disperse. It encompasses the unlimited potential of the divine. Imagine the changes that will take place in your world when each of your hearts is engaged without limitation in the loving practice of embracing all that surrounds you.

Unity consciousness can only be embodied in the fifth dimensional vibration by hearts who love one another, and hearts only love one another when they first love themselves. This is why we spend so much time to share this information with you. As you do your healing work with the lower mind and ego, you become more spiritually alive.

Only in a world where you can, by conscious design, allow every thought, word and deed to manifest the love, trust, grace, faith, compassion and gratitude that resides unconditionally within you, will you inherit the fifth dimension.

We wait here patiently for you.
It is your time now to shine forth.

The Practice of the Evolving Self

Awakened Mastery of the Energies of Love, Trust,
Faith, Compassion, Grace and Gratitude

These exercises are not meant to be done sequentially but
simultaneously. After you have given one day of practice to
each individually, practice them all together throughout the
ongoing days.

Step One - Learn to question yourself.
- Let go of all you "think" you know about yourself.
- Speak the question that springs from the deepest pools
  of your heart.
- Listen with the part of you that is awake enough now
  to hear the answer.

Step Two - Recognize and dismantle your belief systems.
- Be willing to strip away the accumulated layers of illusion hiding "who you think you are" from the real you.
- With compassion, allow all possibilities of creation that
  your human mind has not yet awakened to.
- Develop faith in yourself that you are a master who is capable of co-creating with the universe all that is possible.

*Step Three - Experience a sacred communion with your soul
as a doorway to your GodSelf.*
- Make a list of the belief systems that limit you, and reclaim your energy from them.
- Make another list of what you know, in the depths of
  your heart, to be true about yourself.
- Make a list of judgments you still hold about yourself.

Step Four - a three-fold practice.
- Each morning, upon rising, take some time in solitude
  to contemplate your state of being, honestly and without judgment.
- Throughout the day, work regularly with the energies
  of love, trust, faith, compassion, grace and gratitude.
- Each evening, recognize and embrace in profound hon-
  or all that you have given yourself that day.

Chapter Two

The Heart of Lemuria

Part One - Celestia

Blessings to all who have gathered here today!

We greet you from an energy that is just outside the view of some, but within the hearts of all. With love and respect, honor and divine grace, we join you today to discuss a topic that is the core of our philosophy in Telos.

Our sister Aurelia has requested that we present to you an understanding of the "Heart of Lemuria," and what these energies provide to you in the current time and space in which you find yourself. Much has been spoken about the energy of Lemuria, and much knowledge has been shared about times past. Today our time with you represents a journey into the purest Lemurian energy that exists on the surface of the Earth, the energy that fills and informs your heart.

The "Heart of Lemuria" can be described and illuminated many ways. Inasmuch as you also have these same attributes within your consciousness, you will resonate with this truth. Our brother Ahnahmar will speak to you about the energies of the heart which inspire and build passion for your intended creations. Beloved Adama will speak to you about the Christed energies of the heart, those that connect us with the Divine Source of All That Is.

To begin, as is always the case in birthing a new truth or understanding, I will speak to you of the "feminine" energies of the heart. All sentient beings experience life within the framework of this "great mother" we call Earth and its rhythm to life. It expresses itself through a vibration or frequency that guides us when we are receptive to it. As you tune your heart to the energies of the "great mother," you will gradually start vibrating to her rhythm.

On the surface of the Earth, much emphasis has been given to the qualities of the mind. The pure energy of the heart has been forgotten and replaced with an active extension of the "Intellect" applied to all things. The mind has become an active force in your evolution, rather than the passive structure and tool that was originally intended. The mind's original purpose was to be a faculty in service to the heart, and not the other way around.

In your evolution, most have ignored the promptings of their heart. You have lost your former ability to recognize that the heart is the great intelligence of the soul. The heart knows everything, will always offer the best and highest guidance and will always direct you toward your highest good. For a very long time, you have allowed your human mind to be in service to the ego instead of the heart. The human mind, controlled by the altered ego, has become overly cluttered with fears, judgments and erroneous concepts, and together, they control all your internal programming.

This is why, in abandoning your heart energy long ago and giving priority to the mind, you have created, lifetime after lifetime, a series of painful experiences, poverty and misery. The human mind does not have the wisdom of the heart and is unable to offer you the wisdom of the Mind of God. Only the heart holds that magic key. Originally, the mind was designed to be a receptor of information in service to the heart. It was the heart that knew exactly what to do with the information.

The practice of the "Heart of Lemuria" begins with a return to the origins of your consciousness, wherein the passive mind surrenders to the active heart. As created, the human consciousness expressed itself through an ego, or mind, that was informed directly by the Logos, or Heart of the Divine. The mind itself was a wondrous tool, and was utilized to learn and analyze the myriad sensory inputs that the evolving human experienced. It was the Heart, however, that had the ability to choose the right action and engage in it. Again we say this with much emphasis.

It is the mind's role to learn and analyze.
It is the heart's role to choose and do.
Hearts connect, while minds separate.

This is not a judgment of the role of the mind, but rather the truth of its purpose. In order to analyze, one must differentiate. In order to learn, to acquire intellectual knowledge, one must observe one reality at a time, and quantify or qualify it.

The heart, however, holds the frequency that is open and receptive to all possibilities. It connects us to all that is and does not question or analyze that connection. The heart trusts. It takes in all that is available as a continuous flow, and beats to this rhythm of life with joy and wonder. And from this trust, acceptance and compassion are born. To understand who we are, we must accept what we do. To understand what others are, we must accept what they do. When we truly understand others, how can we fail to love them as fully as they love themselves? How can we not trust them as completely as we trust ourselves?

The heart holds a frequency that is open and receptive to all possibilities. We cannot emphasize this enough: The heart trusts. This frequency is inherent in each and every one of you, whether you choose to recognize it or not. It is not something you need to learn and it is not something you need to analyze in order to create it. It is not something you need to clear a space for, or open your heart wider for. This frequency just IS.

To reiterate what we hear most often here in Telos from you, our Lemurian brothers and sisters, is "When will the veil lift? When will we see you? When will we be able to visit with you in the physical reality in which we currently live?" The answer is: *"It will all happen when your heart is allowed to inform the vibration of your surrendered mind."*

To "lift the veil," the mind must open to all possibilities. To "know" the secrets that exist on the other side of the veil, one must experience through the vibration of the heart. One must simply listen to the frequency that exists within all of us, throughout every instant of creation. You, my beloved sisters and brothers, are the veil. You will continue to be so until your mind surrenders and your heart is allowed to inform your reality.

In Telos, our hearts are open to all possibilities. We teach each other this truth every day. We evolve and understand this truth through our play with each other, each and every day. We are each other's signposts that read "Stop, and open to more possibilities."

On the surface you carry the same heart frequency that we do. Your mind may tell you this is not true, but your heart trusts. Trust is the core energy of the heart. You may feel that your heart has closed itself off from this vibration, or that you cannot feel it in your life or in the people who surround you, but this is not truth. Your heart trusts.

You each form your own boundaries of trust. You form them in the truths you adhere to, in the families, communities and nations you create and experience on the surface. You do not need to deny your boundaries, for they are who you are in this moment. We are here to honor them, for in time, their energies will be transformed through contact with the heart's vibration of trust.

Your minds may not yet own this possibility, but your hearts were created in it. None of you in physical form can disown it because it is the energy that keeps you incarnate. This energy keeps you in the "game of life" that you have chosen, with open and receptive hearts, to participate in.

Now it is time for you to meet with us on the "playing field," so to speak, and engage with us in an exercise of trust.

To begin our play, we must first choose an outward reality that pleases you. We ask each of you to create in your heart's eye the image of a field filled with every creation of Earth that brings you joy. This can include trees and flowers, mountains and streams, birds and animals, nature spirits, crystals, clouds and other humans. Create a field populated by all that you desire to share yourself with. Remember that the frequency of the heart is one of receptivity to all possibilities, so do not constrain yourself.

Now position yourself where you are most comfortable within this field, and begin to observe all that is present around you. Don't observe, however, with the mind. Don't catalog and comment on what you see and hear around you through the mind. Listen instead with the heart; listen for the vibrations and frequencies of the hearts that surround you in all the beings that share the field with you. Recognize the touch of other hearts as they reach out to yours.

At first you will hear/feel/know a gentle energy that comforts and supports you. It cushions you and enfolds you in its warmth and peacefulness. There is quite often a humming noise that accompanies this energy that many of you hear with your physical ears. This is the joint energy of all your hearts in combination with the heart of the Earth. It is the energy of trust that informs the Earth, you, us, and every being that resides here.

Rest in this energy for as long as you wish! Get to know it as you would your own bed at home. Get to know it as you would your own skin. The more you connect in with this energy and make it a part of your everyday existence, the easier it will be to hear the frequency of your own heart, and the sooner you will begin to speak its language of trust.

Experience this energy in your physical existence, as well as your multi-dimensional bodies. It is most important at this juncture in the planet's evolution that all experiences be brought into the physical realm. You must ground this new reality in your cellular structure. It is not enough to know this in your "higher selves," so to speak. It is imperative that your DNA record this new identity in all of your various bodies. This is a goal that each of you set for yourself in this lifetime.

Now, as you float on and within this cushion of energy, begin to listen to the frequency of all the hearts that surround you. Each plays a subtle tune which is distinct from the rest. As you begin to recognize the signature of each heart's song, you can follow that song back to the heart from which it originates. Do this with trust and tenderness, and you will find only trust.

You are rediscovering the language that you originally spoke. You are rediscovering a form of communication that connects you directly with all life around you. It will not take long this time to speak it again. The frequency is as close as your own heart. Simply call to your heart and it will guide you.

Stay in this field and return to it as often as you wish, until the cushion of heart energy is so familiar that to step out of it brings immediate recognition. Return until there is no place to return to because this field is now your daily frame of existence.

Allow your mind to wander in this field. Let it surrender itself, in trust, to all possibilities. This may be a bit tricky at first, as the mind will want to label and define what it sees. Your task now is to accept the mind, the structure of the mind, and allow it to join you in this field. Allow it to play, but watch it as you would a child who is venturing out into the world and does not yet know what to expect. Remind it of your heart's frequency and receptivity to all possibilities. Invite your mind to play with possible realities, and not just those which hold a sense of familiarity.

Within this field is your connection to us. This field exists beyond any veils. Let your mind surrender and your heart do the choosing. We will always be here to meet you. With a welcoming heart, I leave you now and ask our beloved Ahnahmar to guide your journey.

Part Two - Ahnahmar

I greet you all with the prospect of much enjoyment between us. Our discussion of the heart has brought you to a greater understanding of one aspect of the energies we refer to as the "Heart of Lemuria." Whereas my sister Celestia held forth on the subject of receptivity in the heart, I now wish to speak to you of the relationship between the heart's energy and the point of light we call creation.

It is through passion and intention that all is created in your world and ours. Energy and frequency gather in complementary networks. The grid of electro-magnetic energies called by many, including us, "lattice energy," holds the structure of universal energy. It is through this grid that all beings present themselves to the Universe.

27

We communicate our intentions by using our own heart energy *(our passion)* to inform the "scalar" energies that hold the complementary frequency. These scalar waves fill the void within the grid-work.

This process of creation is then enjoined with the focus of the mind or ego, so that a singular event may be extended out from the totality of the whole. The extension then takes form in the physical plane, and becomes a reality in human consciousness.

Creation indeed takes place the moment that your human consciousness first becomes aware of it. With each and every thought, the energies of the lattice and the scalar meet to form a point of light that is then expanded, if you so desire. This cycle of heart—to mind—to heart is lightning fast, and much of the time you are not even aware of it. For many, it has become a case of the chicken and the egg, for there is confusion as to what starts the process, the heart or the mind. On the surface, much credence has been given to the mind as instigator.

I will say to you that the heart is always the creator. In the pool of wisdom that is the heart resides true inspiration for all that surrounds you. The heart's language is more subtle; however, it is often even timid, for you have not given much support to the heart's frequency in your dimension. In truth, the high incidence of heart disease on your plane is a direct symptom of this, as is most other disease.

To understand the process, this cycle of creation, we must recognize another aspect of heart energy, that of active intention. We call this intention "passion." In your dimension, most of the credit for "inspiration" has been given to the mind. The mind has been given leadership over all aspects of your consciousness.

In your world, this leadership of the mind over the heart

has led to strife, both internal and external; for the leadership of the mind leads to separation instead of unity. Yet the mind is a necessary tool in the process of creation, so then how do we reconcile this? To return to full consciousness, as divine beings, it is imperative that you now begin to turn the leadership over to the heart, and allow it to rule rather than the mind.

How does this happen in practical terms? First you must develop a greater understanding of the nature of the mind. It exists in human consciousness as two minds, which we will term the higher mind and the lower mind. The higher mind is a center for inspiration, for it is directly in touch with both your heart and the divine mind.

The higher mind is itself a center of receptivity, storing all impressions and experiences that you encounter in your evolution. The higher mind inevitably feels a pressure to grasp more than it is responsible for. It suffers a need to understand all that is presented to it, and to find a resolution for it. Yet it cannot, for resolution is found only through the heart.

The first step is to practice patience in the higher mind. Allow this part of your mind to relax, to observe and to communicate to your heart its impressions and the inspiration it receives from the divine mind. Accept its process and do not try to "turn off the mind," as so many practices instruct you to do. In order to achieve this, one must ease the focus on the mind and relax its responsibility to "do" something. It is the heart energy that is responsible for this, although not by doing, but by "being."

The lower mind has its own set of tools for your evolution. It is the research center for your existence and is always focused and busy. While the higher mind is a bridge between the heart and the divine mind, the lower mind is the bridge between the heart and the mental plane. The lower mind is the cataloger of all that you take in on the physical plane.

The mind is not designed to surrender. The mind represents the computer that runs your internal programming. It is a wondrous tool with great potential for processing and sharing your human experiences. And yet, the lower mind is not the place from which to choose or to make decisions. It is not the authority on how to "do" or "be" in your life. Your heart is the only authority.

The second step becomes a daily practice of separating yourself from the chatter of your lower mind. This practice will allow your consciousness to listen for the more subtle frequency of your heart's wisdom.

A simple and yet effective method for achieving this is to direct your awareness to the sound of your heartbeat.

Divert your attention away from the voice of your lower mind and listen until you can feel and hear the beat of your heart throughout your entire body. If you need to, physically place your fingers over a pulse point on your body until you can feel the rhythm. Then enter into this rhythmic flow until you feel at one with the center of your being.

Removing control from the mind allows the original frequency stored in your cells to remind you of "who you are," and lets the energies of other hearts remind you of "why you are here." A return to the frequency of the heart reconnects you to the energy of the Divine which can guide you to remember who you are and return you to full consciousness.

You have all become extremely proficient at pondering with the mind, and you have all perfected the art of intellectual evaluation and judgment. In so doing, however, you have permitted an energetic gap to form between yourselves and all that surrounds you. Now is the time to remember and relearn to think with the heart. This form of receptivity is connective, energetically rhythmic and infinitely more attentive to the physical self.

It is within the physical self that you have chosen to experience and learn. You carry with you a cellular template, a lineage of all that you are, including your Lemurian lineage. Your Lemurian self is stored in the energetic memory of your heart. Each of you has an energy template that is unique and yet part of the whole. The information that you seek with your mind regarding your Lemurian heritage is stored in your very cells. Yet, many of you seek to exit this physical storehouse of energy and information about yourself.

You seek to leave your physical incarnation and ascend to another realm where the travails of physicality will not assail you. Yet we say to you with all certainty, that you need to transcend the separation you feel resides within the physical body that you have ceased to love.

Heart energy keeps you in incarnation. The information of the heart allows you to reconnect the physical with the spiritual. It is the animating force that connects your soul with all other souls. Your heartbeat tunes you to the collective cellular memory that recalls the spiritual paradise you believe you have lost, while in truth, you have never lost it. You have only created a veil, as our beloved Celestia stated, behind which you give your authority away to the mind which is no longer open to all possibilities.

Choosing from the heart, living from the heart instead of the mind, is a collective, connective action that restores the memory of the love of being alive. It celebrates the wonder and gift of physicality with guidance from a sentient heart. It returns all life to a "doing" that does not try to make things happen as the mind does, but allows you to be available and receptive to all that exists, including the passion that is your natural birthright. For this, my cherished sisters and brothers, is the true "heart of the matter." It is the heart of *all* matter.

Physical life, the solidness that has been created in your

dimension, is not devoid of light. It is not darker because it is denser than the dimension in which we reside. It is darker because you have lost your love for it. You have concluded that another place, another dimension, is where you desire to be, withdrawing your passion from the plane in which you exist. Without this passion, this energy of the heart, you have lost the connection with your Divine Essence. You have transferred authority to others, to masters whom you believe to be more evolved and more enlightened than you. You have made us in Telos your gods, much as the ancient Romans and Greeks did. But we are not any different than you are.

All that we are resides within your cells as well. The only difference is that we recognize it fully and love it unconditionally. We also share it with all those surrounding us. We speak to each other from our hearts, and we store and imprint our hearts with all experiences for ourselves and for our lineage.

We follow a practice of "being" which differs from those primarily "mind" techniques that many of you use. What we do is not based on meditation. You could call it allowing ourselves to "contemplate" rather than to meditate. And we reach with our practices very high levels of heightened awareness. What we practice is not based on visualization or imagery techniques either, which still require mental effort, and place the emphasis on something you are not rather than something you are. For example, we contemplate the infinite aspects of our divinity in order to raise our vibration to higher levels and integrate those new truths we constantly discover about ourselves.

We start by becoming silent and still enough to listen to our own hearts beat. We lighten the attention of our minds and let the mind talk to itself for a while. Then we allow our receptivity to expand to all that is around us. We don't tune out the world around us, but instead tune in with all of our senses by becoming one with the flow that is around us and within us.

The heart has its own emotional intellect. It senses and records all that impacts it. As it becomes entrained to the gentle energetic waves of nature, with the physical world around it, we know with complete consciousness that we have contacted the world through our heart.

We allow the heart lessons that are around us in every moment to inform us, and we store them in our cellular memory. We shift time, for when the heart is tuned to its inherent frequency in the present moment and in the flow of "All That Is," self, time and space are united in oneness.

Lastly, we send our heart lessons out to the world around us. For in truth, this is the true act of creation. It is the true "doing" and "being" which informs all of our existence and yours. The inspiration and the passion of the heart are bonded to the inspiration and passion of the Divine. The attention of the mind is then focused on it, for where awareness goes, so goes the energy to sustain it. And finally, the creation is anchored into the cellular template of the physical wherein it takes form. The point of light that blossoms at the intersection of soul touching soul, of heart energy touching heart energy, receives true expression in the physical world.

Follow this practice of heart and mind. Allow your being and your consciousness to connect with the Heart of Lemuria once again, and you will find yourself in the paradise that you are yearning for.

We greet you as always, with our hearts open and receptive to all the possibilities that exist in your dimension and ours. We offer our support in assisting you to remember your real identity, and who you have always been. With love and blessings until we meet again, I now turn you over to our beloved Adama.

Part Three - Adama

Blessings to all in attendance today! I beckon you to the halls of the Great Temple of Knowledge in Telos. Contained within its walls is the library of our Lemurian lineage, a storehouse of experience in crystalline form. These crystals come in all shapes, colors and sizes, and each has its own frequency in order to best represent and express the information it holds.

I invite you here today so that you may recognize the truth of the vibration of this place, for it is a mirror of you. It is a duplicate of the temple that resides within your physical body, in the crystalline cellular structure that you inhabit and maintain. Within your field of consciousness, I ask you in this moment to connect with the energy of the crystal grid of planet Earth, so that we may all be connected together as we continue our exploration of the Heart of Lemuria.

Today, I wish to speak with you on the nature of forgiveness, which is the greatest truth one can derive from the practice of the Heart of Lemuria. Forgiveness is the nature of the Creator and the Divine.

One of the key aspects of spiritual and emotional nourishment is forgiveness. Even deeper than that is the level of Divinity which recognizes, states and lives the truth that there is nothing to forgive. You cannot create this truth; you can only discover it. You have an opportunity now to learn this truth for yourselves, and our great Earth mother has the opportunity to live this truth with all of us.

Many of you have reached a place on your spiritual path where the trauma of past experiences has brought you to a juncture. This crossroad holds anger, grief, sorrow and shame on one side, and joy, wisdom, love, creativity and truth on the other.

Shame is the illusion that there is something you can do, or someone else can do to you, which is wrong and for which there is no possible redemption or forgiveness. You have been taught this as a society and as a race. You have been taught this through most religious traditions and belief systems.

But the truth is that in the past, events happened that you didn't have the wisdom at the time to understand. There are no victims in our dimension or in yours. We all chose to incarnate here and experience the full spectrum of the physical expression of the Divine. We are all Divine expressions of the Creator experiencing being and consciousness for eternity. Our desire for experience has encompassed every facet of the godhead.

When we first incarnated as god beings and as creator gods, our experience was very close to that of the Creator. In the beginning, the veil separating us from the Creator was the thinnest possible. But then souls became interested in deviating or distancing themselves from the experience of being the creator, wanting a deeper experience of "not being God" so that they could gain a greater understanding of what it is to "be God."

Through these experiences we created more and more "unknowingness," and more and more confusion. Over a long period of time, we moved into realms in which we chose higher and higher levels of suffering, as we followed an exploration of individual soul paths. Each individual soul is on a greater soul path, which is the aspect that the creator is most interested in understanding, such as joy.

The soul will choose to have all the experiences needed to understand this aspect. These experiences usually express themselves as a lack of that aspect, as opposed to the experience of it. One who wishes to understand the importance and purpose of joy chooses incarnations in which they have a joyless existence.

All of these experiences we have chosen have become a part of our cellular memories. They became patterns in our genetic information. Together our genetic lineage became a part of the fabric of the Earth's heart and soul, for her evolution and her ascension have also been a part of our journey. From incarnation to incarnation, throughout all the civilizations of Earth, we have traveled this path. We have experienced cataclysm and redemption. We have created density of physicality and witnessed miracles. We have walked this Earth as Masters of Light and Love and as slaves of violent emotions. We have all been healers and we have all been murderers. It is time to forgive ourselves for all that we have done, and all that has been done in our name.

Now is the time to connect again to the pure frequency of your heart, the Heart of Lemuria, the heart of the Divine. For within this frequency lies the essence of forgiveness, and within the essence of forgiveness lies the truth of your Divine Essence.

We have witnessed so many of you crying out that you are still trapped behind the veil, that you cannot be in touch with your family and friends on the other side of the veil. You complain that you are not allowed to gather with us and share in our lifestyle and community, which seems to include more ease and grace than the one you currently live in. But I will say to you again that the only veil that exists is the one you have created. The veil that you still experience is the veil of your fears, your erroneous belief systems and your sadness.

It is not the traumas you have suffered over the course of your evolution that are the cause of your pain today; it is your unwillingness to feel your pain. It is your unwillingness to experience the fear and sadness and nourish your pain with forgiveness. The act of forgiving the self is what brings you back to the pure frequency of the Heart of Lemuria. Rather than embracing your pain, you long for things to be otherwise; you turn from your pain rather than towards it.

Give yourself permission to feel again and to rediscover the heart's vibration. Where most of you are now emotionally, behind the veil, your fears often feel like they will cause your heart to stop or beat faster and faster. The sorrows and sadness you hold within cause the heart to feel as though it would break in physical terms. Offer God your broken heart if you wish and allow the Divine within your Sacred Heart to bring a healing.

In truth, it is your mind that is taking you deeper into the reservoir of emotion than you have encountered throughout your lifetimes. But the mind alone cannot accomplish this type of healing. The heart's frequency is what guides us through this seeming minefield and nourishes us with the love of the Universe.

Each time you give permission for this to happen, you are connecting to your cellular memory again. You can move the fear or the sadness out of your physical structure and out of your DNA's genetic lineage for all time and space.

You may begin to feel your body in ways you have not experienced before. It can be a general feeling of comfort or more connection to the body, where it becomes more graceful, more energetic or experiences a decrease of pain. This release can manifest in a certain part of the body, such as in an organ, a muscle or the skeletal system.

The frequency of forgiveness resonates with the frequency of the heart. Tapping into the heart allows you to inform the mind and the body of this gift, not just for this lifetime, but for all lifetimes. Many have written that the soul is located in the central cell of the pineal gland. This is not exact. In truth, the body lies within the soul. What we call the aura is its lowest vibration. The soul extends outward around the body. Our souls create the energy that motivates the body to move on. The soul defines our level of health or sickness.

It is through the heart's frequency that we connect with our soul, and with the soul of the Divine of which we are all a part. The best tonic for all maladies of the heart, all disconnection from this divine frequency and the rhythm of your physical life, is forgiveness.

The most powerful way to nourish each other is to listen to another person's truth and accept it. The next level is hearing another person's truth, accepting them for what they are, and loving them for it. The next level is hearing another's truth, accepting them and loving them in spite of it. This is the essence of forgiveness that, truthfully, there is nothing to forgive.

The heart that beats in your body is the same as the Heart of Lemuria.

Listen to it and treasure it. You are not incomplete and you are not incapable of becoming this Heart with your entire being and vibrating with this frequency throughout your beingness. When you become this, no other initiations or purifications will be necessary before you can be allowed to pass through the veil.

All you need, all you have ever needed, lies within you. It is only your awareness of it that must shift, not through the mind but through the heart, which will mirror this frequency to the world around you.

Your awareness has been focused until now on the veil of duality, which was created by the nature of the mind, not that of the heart. The mind's awareness will always seek to qualify and differentiate, to judge one against the other. It will see anger and distrust, because it also sees love and calm. It will see arrogance and greed because it also sees mercy and generosity.

The heart, however, is aware only of unity, which is the product of unconditional love and forgiveness. Forgiveness is what will allow you to stop avoiding the pain that has been there for so long. The light of awareness will enter into the parts of your soul that have long been relegated to the shadows, and you will no longer be able to deny yourselves entry into the Heart of Lemuria that exists around you without veil at all times. And what will it be like to awaken free of all veils? Free of judgment and remorse? Free of fear and sadness? Free of the desire for everything and anything to be different? Free of the feelings of shame and unworthiness? Free of the illusion that you are not God?

It will be like your heart has burst into a realm of infinite possibility and infinite joy. You will discover that everything you have ever desired has been there all along. The world around you will hold this same frequency, and we will be there to greet you!

May the love of the Divine show itself to each of you in the vibration of your heart! And may the Heart of Lemuria shine on Earth through all dimensions of time and space! This is our greatest wish for you today. We thank each of you for entertaining this possibility and for joining with us in love and unity.

Until we speak again, I am your friend and brother, Adama.

Give yourself permission to feel again
And to rediscover the heart's vibration.
Where most of you are now, behind the veil,
Your fears feel like they will
Cause your heart to stop or beat faster.
And the sorrows and sadness
You hold within it cause the heart
To feel as though it is breaking.
Offer God your broken heart if you wish,
And allow the Divine
Within your Sacred Heart
To bring a healing.
- Adama

Chapter Three

Assignment from Adama to Aurelia

Dialogue between Sananda and Aurelia

Sananda - How are you today, my beloved?

Aurelia - *Much better, things are opening up step by step.*

Sananda - And what are you ready for now?

Aurelia - *I'm ready for the next step.*

Sananda - Big adventures ahead of you! Are you ready?

Aurelia - *Big adventures all right. They are opening out in front of me all the time. I think I am ready. Before it would have scared me; now I feel different about it and I think it is going to be a lot of fun.*

Sananda - What can I do for you in this now moment?

Aurelia - *I need your help to get through something I feel stuck with and have much resistance to. There is something I don't understand. Adama has been helping me every week towards my next step. He has been giving me assignments to do, which I have been doing, but this week, he gave me an assignment that I feel great resistance to doing.*

Sananda - Those are the best ones.

Aurelia - *Well, he said that it is a very important one and I want to do it. I thought you could give me more clarity. He told me to name ten people I don't like or have had the most problems with in my life. He suggested that I remember that we are all one, and look for how those people are part of me and how I am also part of them. He wants me to start seeing the Oneness and Unity that we have with each other.*

This does not resonate with me too well because I feel I am my own person. I don't feel that I am them and that they are me. He asked me to spend an hour and a half with each person, bringing them into my heart and creating the spirit of oneness and unity with them. I have a difficult time even imagining that if I succeed in spending an hour and a half with each person with whom I have no affinity, I am going to come to the conclusion that they are me and that we are the same.

Sananda - And you are asking me for my advice?

Aurelia - *Well, hmmm ... of course! I am hoping that you can tell me something else that might help me to get through this assignment.*

Sananda - Here is my advice. Leave everything you are doing now, and do this assignment immediately, completely and thoroughly to the very core of your being. Adama suggested this because if you do this, you will enter the world of Oneness. This is your next step, your next initiation and the one that will allow you to enter into union with self. You cannot enter into union as long as you feel a rift with anybody or with any part of life, including all those with whom you have had problems.

Entering into union means being in Oneness with every part of life and honoring the level of divinity they represent.

This includes entering into union and great honoring with the animal kingdom, the nature kingdom, and many more of which you are not yet aware. Union, as it is understood in the fifth dimension, comprises the oneness with all that exists, not just with one part of it. It includes union with the Creator Supreme, with the Holy Mother Earth, the sentience of this planet, union with the I AM Presence, the totality of your being, union with all parts of yourself and with all kingdoms of the Earth, known and unknown, the animal kingdom, also including all the elements of air, fire, water and earth.

When this level of union is fully attained in your consciousness, you are then invited to come through the portals of the fifth dimension and receive the glorious crowning of your long journey on Earth. With great ceremony and honoring, you will be drenched in the ascension fires and you will emerge totally transformed. You will then join the immortals forever. You will be with us, dear one, face to face, working at our side in full consciousness, and never again will you know any level of limitation.

Adama knows what he is doing; I suggest that you take his advice very seriously. As you know, Adama and I work together very closely in the light realm. We have known each other forever, and we are both working very closely with you to assist you in your next step. You know that I consider myself a Lemurian as part of my identity.

With the original Aurelia, Adama and several others from our home planet Lemur in the Land of Mu, I was among the first ones to incarnate on this planet, a very long time ago, to be part of the new Lemurian race that came here to create Christ consciousness. We all came together, a unified group, from the Land of Mu of the Dahl's universe, in the great ship I once told you about. Of course, I am not limited to this identity exclusively. Like everyone else, I am expanded in multitudes of other ways as well.

Adama is an awe-inspiring ascended master, and he loves you so very much. He is doing all he can to assist you to finally understand the vibration of the fifth dimension, so that you can become it, and "enter into this world of Oneness." It is a process. Do not allow yourself to become impatient with yourself, as it will hold you back. Remember what Ahnahmar has told you about expectations!

No need to mention how much joy your beloved Ahnahmar is feeling in his heart to see you coming so close to your "homecoming." There are no words in your dimension to describe the love that Ahnahmar holds for you. You will be so happy when you take the final step. What I say to you now, I also say to all those who have applied to become a candidate for ascension. They will have to walk the same path you are on now. The more you engage in creating this pathway toward ascension, the easier it will be for others to do the same. Many of you are way-showers, beacons of Light, preparing the way for others who will follow.

Aurelia - That is what Adama told me.

Sananda - Now you are hearing it twice. Will you be checking with another master just to be sure?

Aurelia - Probably! (Giggle) *My problem is that I have some difficulty accepting and integrating that I am really one with the people I don't like. I realize that we all come from the same Creator, but that we are all the same and all one, is just not my cup of tea.*

Sananda - You feel this way because you do not yet see the real truth and wisdom you need to embrace to make your next step with ease and grace. You have not yet taken this wisdom to the deeper level you need to receive the full understanding. So let us work with this for a moment, because it is important that everyone present, and all those who will be reading your book, understand this well for themselves.

You will all need this wisdom eventually and I want to share with everyone this important teaching.

Understand that there is a reason you don't like those individuals and you have had some unpleasant encounters with them. There may have been some abrasiveness perhaps, or they may have rubbed you the wrong way. They may have been a kind of irritant in your life, such as someone trying to exploit you, etc. Now, take that irritation and identify it. Ask yourself what is it about that person that really irritates me, annoys me or makes me angry?

Ask yourself what emotions come up inside you. How do you feel about yourself in the presence of the person? It will become evident that this person makes you feel a certain way you do not like. Well, of course, they cannot make you feel anything negative, because they do not have that power. You alone have this power. If you feel an irritation, it is because the emotions are already present within you.

These people on your list act as a trigger and your mirror for you to recognize what you still have to heal within yourself to move to a higher vibrational frequency. It really has nothing to do with the other person. Now, dig deep, really look inside yourself and analyze how you are feeling, and how other people and other experiences in your life have triggered the very same issues. Look through your life for how many times this has occurred, perhaps not in exactly the same manner, but in a similar way.

Aurelia - Hundreds of times perhaps.

Sananda - Indeed! Then ask yourself the question, what have I judged or hated within myself that has created this mirror? You know very well that it is all about you, about how you feel about yourself on the deepest of levels. It is never about the other person. When you really go deep, you will come to understand that this merely represents a misunderstanding, a judgment you have held about yourself or anger you have held within yourself. It is about a false belief you have created about yourself. When you heal a rift with another person, it is not the other person you are healing; it is yourself. The other person may or may not benefit; that is not your concern. You are the main character creating your own healing.

These experiences are catalysts that you create because you want to resolve the false beliefs you hold about yourself, those buried deep within the subconscious or unconscious minds. They are created from higher perspective to trigger a new level of healing. God is not sending you people to annoy you for his own entertainment. You, yourself, through your own divine intent to realize your enlightenment, magnetically attract those individuals who will provoke your own limitations and bring them to the surface of conscious awareness, to help you experience what needs to be healed. From such experience, you will be able to make new choices for yourself.

When you face a mirror, first identify your feelings and go deeply into them. The persons triggering the mirror do not really intend to annoy you; they are just being who they are. When you decide you no longer want to feel this false belief about yourself, you begin to change the false identity. You start perceiving your own worth and acknowledge that you are greater in worth and value than the mirrors that were presented to you. And in deep emotion, in deep love and acceptance, you choose a new identity for yourself. As you continue to align and heal the false beliefs you hold about yourself, interesting miracles occur in your life. The world around you adjusts to your new identity.

The next time you are in the presence of the person, there will be no energy; it will be completely gone because you have handled the issue within yourself. Now, another way you can resolve something when you face a mirror is to ask yourself, how am I that also? Be willing to experience the mirror within according to your own uniqueness. Let us say, for example, you witness someone lying or stealing something. If this annoys you, ask yourself the question, how am I that also?

Perhaps you are not a thief and you simply cannot relate to what is going on, but the irritation is there. It could be that you have stolen from yourself in very subtle ways. The thief is simply a trigger. The mirror image may not always be exact, but it will always relate to self. How have I done this to myself also?

Aurelia - I have a real issue around this, and here it is. If I have to make peace and consider as "myself" the people who have tried to control me or derail my mission, and you well know who some of them are, my fear is that they will try to come back in my life again to annoy me and mess up things again. I have a peaceful life now and I don't want to lose it.

Sananda - Did you hear me tell you to make peace with them?

Aurelia - No.

Sananda - As I told you before, it is not about them, but about you and your relationship with self. You can only do the inner work within yourself and make peace with yourself. You can rarely make peace with another person in the mirror game, because you will find that they most likely perceive everything very differently than you do. You can only heal yourself, and they can only heal themselves. They are not your responsibility.

It really does not matter whether you see those people ever again or not. It is not about approaching them and healing everything with them, because this desire could be a projection. If they want to heal themselves they can do the job themselves. That is their choice. Your responsibility is to heal yourself and move on in vibration into Oneness. Bless them, send them love and release them.

Aurelia - Ok, that is the key I was missing, and I am getting this now more clearly.

Sananda - Yes, I said that when you heal the feeling within yourself, the next time you encounter the individual, no energy reaction will be triggered. This does not mean that you are going to make peace with them or that you will have to become engaged with their energies again. Healing your side of it does not create further obligations.

Aurelia - Sometimes you have to work with them and face them in your daily life, in a work setting, or they may live in your house or neighborhood.

Sananda - No, it is never about them, it is about you; they are just the trigger or the mirror. And if you reject the mirror, your own Divine Essence will send you another one, and perhaps a more unpleasant one. Not because Adama has made this suggestion, but because it is appropriate in the timing in your evolution right now. It is your own Divine Essence who wills this for you at this time.

Aurelia - I am asking about this is because I want to get through with Adama's assignment. I want to do a thorough job and understand it better.

Sananda - You are going to find that this will be most joyful and very empowering. Now, there are some instances when you may want or have to actually interact with a person who has been a trigger for you, but do it only after you have given yourself your full healing. If you approach them before, it could be disastrous. There are times when you may wish to approach the person, especially if there are hurt feelings involved. You may want to apologize for something. I am not saying you should, but your heart will know what to do. You will always have a feeling and a sense of what is right, of what is aligned and appropriate.

For the most part, these mirror experiences are solely for you in your relationship with self. Each time you work with this type of annoying experience and you attain a greater state of enlightenment within yourself, you bring yourself closer and closer to Oneness. You begin to feel Oneness with all things and no longer take your life experiences or your encounters so personally.

You realize you created the experience, and you will own it with ease. When you are faced with a strange, awkward or challenging mirror in the form of a person in your life, you will be able to say right away, "I created that, I attracted that experience to myself. I know that I did this to create an important healing for myself, and I accept this lesson with profound gratitude."

So, this is all about restoring your dignity, finding your deepest truths, becoming more empowered and getting clear. As you practice this process, you will find that when you have done it, you will not attract these kinds of mirrors anymore. The mirrors you will attract will become quite different, positively reflecting your healed state. Mirrors are not only negative, you know, they reflect the full spectrum, as does everything else.

Aurelia - The way you are explaining this teaching to me now is very helpful. You have explained this many times before; it is not the first time I have heard this. I am getting this understanding much more clearly. I can now do this assignment with more confidence. Thank you, Sananda.

Sananda - You are welcome, beloved, and Adama will help you. This is a profound choice and suggestion that he has made for your advancement, and he will help you through the entire process.

When you can simply look at everything around you in the world, and state and feel within yourself that you are all of this also, you will know what it is to be God. When you meet your Creator, this is exactly what he will say to you: "I am you and you are me; we are the same. All that you have done, I have done also, because I have done it with you. We are one and the same."

Owning, beloved, is the greatest power of all.
Owning in equality with Self will bring
miracles upon miracles in your life.

Aurelia - I shall do it thoroughly.

Sananda - So be it. You will be forever happy that you did so. This is another fifth dimensional protocol that everyone will experience, passing through the same initiatic process you are now involved in, to enter into Oneness.

Aurelia - Thank you very much. I am most grateful for your assistance at this time.

Sananda - You are welcome, beloved.

Part of this channeling with Sananda took place with the assistance of Eterna (Linda Bandino), now in Mount Shasta, channel for Sananda for many years.

www.revelations.org (Eterna's contact)

Chapter Four

The Dark Night of the Heart

Last Steps of Initiation for Final Admission to the Fifth Dimension

Dialogue between Aurelia, Adama and Ahnahmar

Adama - I greet you with the love of my heart and the wisdom of my soul. How are you today, my beloved?

Aurelia - I am well enough, but I feel fatigued in my physical body, and to some extent I still feel the dark night of the Heart, which I have been going through for quite some time. I still feel much pain in my heart center and within my body in spite of all the work I have done to heal myself in the last several years. This is becoming old and tiring. How much longer will it take to heal and be well again, to rejuvenate and all the rest?

Adama - You are one right now who holds a very big piece on this planet. You hold a great deal of energy for humanity and for the ascension of Earth. This accounts for some of your pains. You have done this for a very long time, but now is the time when so much is at stake, and you are doing much work on the inner planes at night as well. This is why you wake up tired in the morning. You need more rest than you are allowing yourself to take.

Aurelia - Yes, but there is so much to do and so many demands on my time; the days seem too short. *Unless I do what I do, the Lemurian mission would not be expanding the way it is. It is exploding in several countries, not just the USA, and many are now beginning to join in.*

Adama - We understand that you are exhausted by this long journey, and it is time for you to make the last steps of your final initiation to ascension. You are almost there, but you are holding back. In certain ways, you are hanging on to many third dimensional patterns and vibrations; unless you let go completely of those patterns, you cannot go any further in your ascension process. If you apply yourself to the final leap in consciousness which we will discuss with you today, you can be "home" very quickly. Never again will you feel tired, the struggles you are feeling now will be gone and you will step out of limitation.

You are much closer than you think. As always, the last steps are the most difficult and often the most painful ones. Every master who has ever ascended from this plane has had to go through the same initiations you are now going through; this includes all of us in Telos and in the fifth dimensional Lemuria.

You are being called to world service and to do much traveling. As you travel, you will be taking with you and offering to many their first experience of this new energy. You must purify yourself as you travel; you must stay within your highest self and never allow anything to upset you. You must especially not allow your ego to react, no matter what you see or experience, and regardless of the way some people may treat you. Never again be tempted to become bitter, resentful or judgmental of anything or anyone. These are the attitudes and energies that keep you glued to third dimension experiences.

You now carry a very high-energy frequency for all those

who meet you; we want you to know this. This is an energy that will work for you in wondrous ways. The more you stay in this energy, the more you will be in the embrace of your divinity, and the more it will support you. Fill yourself each day with as much Light as you can hold. If you take an energetic dive into a vibration that does not blend well with this energy, you will tire easily. You will then recognize the need to realign your energy field again.

It is time for you to make a conscious effort to stay within this energy daily, hourly and around the clock. Most of what I say to you applies to all those who will be reading this material. They will eventually have to walk the same path you are now walking, though it will unfold differently for each one.

This energy we speak of is the feminine energy that you call Mother Mary. We suggest that, each day, you ask her to come into your energy field. Ask for her energy to stay with you throughout the day, to guide you as she holds you in her embrace. Can you do this?

Aurelia - *Yes.*

Adama - There are times when energies will come up for you that will create within you a need for release. These energies will have a vibration of sadness, or disease or grief with what is happening around you and in the world. But again, each time you feel these energies, turn them over to Mary. She will clear them for you. It is her heartfelt desire to assist you. Can you do this?

Aurelia - *Yes.*

Adama - We ask you to do this because much energy is going to be shared with you on your upcoming trip and other trips you will be taking in the future. The energy will be much more intense than in the past. You are capable of receiving this increased energy. You are going to be doing your traveling this time from a higher level of vibration than when you have traveled before. You are ready to enter this level now, but to do so, you must stay in balance yourself. It is very important that you recognize your own energy in this and that you recognize how much control you have over what takes place during your travels.

There is a fine line between your recognition of what you can do for yourself and what is to be turned over. In any moment when you feel your energy begin to falter, you will know that you can raise your vibration immediately or you will know that this is something you are to turn over. This will be a great new exploration.

The six weeks that you journey will give you much experience in learning to work with your own energies, in learning to work with what is creating the fatigue that is hindering you on your mission. But you must trust this; you must understand that you do have this ability. Learn to manage your own energy and use your discernment to determine whether you are depleted by someone else's energy. You are now finally learning to work with your own vibration in a new way, as are many of those with whom you will come in contact. Is this clear?

Aurelia - *Yes. I will do my best.*

Adama - And recognize that when you meet a situation beyond what you are capable of in the moment, turn it over to the higher realm. Never try to resolve it by yourself without the assistance of your team; they are here to support you. Use them wisely and without hesitation. When you feel their energies coming to support you and you feel your own energies expanding, move forward. If for some reason you experience energies or situations beyond your control that are not supporting you, know these are not within your power to resolve by yourself, and turn them over to us.

Aurelia - I have planned the trip as best I could, with as much detail as possible in this dimension, but I also know that it may not unfold the way I have planned.

Adama - We would say to you that the particulars of the trip will unfold as you have set them up, but in reality, that is not the real trip. The real trip is all that will be presented to you that you do not yet know. We suggest that you remain open to this. You must remain open to those who will contact you as you have in the past. The contacts you have made without your total awareness have often been the most important and the most intense for you, and some of them have become the most heartfelt and long-lasting. The same will be true on this trip. You will meet many people you have a heart connection with. Also recognize that you are a spokesman for these energies, and the more you embody them, the more you will be able to share them with others to assist them on their journey.

Aurelia - You think I am ready for all this?

Adama - We know that you are ready, but it is important for you to know this as well. Trust yourself. We would say that any time you feel you are not ready, we invite you to turn that feeling over to us.

The faith is what holds you in that energy. Each time you experience an energy, a small voice saying to you: "I do not feel adequate for this," or something similar, turn it over. It is time for you to realize that there is a great difference between the energies coming from your heart and its vibration, and the thoughts of inadequacy and judgment from your mind, which can trick you. The more you can acknowledge what is not you, the more you will stay in the vibration that you seek. You will make a fifth dimensional journey this time, if you choose. It is for you to open yourself to that opportunity and to feel responsible for staying in balance. This is the time now for everyone to fully understand what it means and what it takes to stay in balance with the new energies flooding the planet. This is how, with each supportive choice you make, you are gaining in your mastery.

Aurelia - Should I seek to spend more time alone?

Adama - The time you spend alone is always valuable. We hope that you recognize, on this third trip, you cannot give yourself over completely like you have often done in the past. You need to take time for yourself to recharge your inner battery. Find places you can go on your own without other people following you. Take time for yourself, to walk the streets by yourself, to be with people and to be out in the towns that you are visiting. Go by yourself whenever it is appropriate. It is very important because it gives you two opportunities. The first, the most important, is to understand your own energy, The second is for you to share this energy with others who would not necessarily come to the gatherings that you are hosting. The time has come for you to walk in the world.

Aurelia - That's a big thing for me. I have always avoided traveling, particularly in cities and crowded places.

Adama - And it is a wonderful thing. In truth, as you begin to walk, you will find the energy you have been lacking. The lack of energy you experience is due largely to the fact that you are no longer in an energy that supports you. It is time to walk and integrate the energies that do. Each time a situation comes up that causes you to worry, or that you have pain over, give it to God. As I say these things to Aurelia, I also say them to all those reading this material. At this time, she represents all of you, and you all can learn from her experiences. You all have more or less the same problems and issues.

Aurelia - I don't understand one statement you just made: that I am no longer walking in the energy that supports me. Can you explain this further?

Adama - You are not.

Aurelia - *I don't understand that.*

Adama - You have moved into higher vibration energy, at least a large part of you has; yet there is a part of you which feels the need to remain in the old energies. This is not to say that you are going to be leaving Mount Shasta or that you are leaving the work you are now doing. You can do all of this in the fifth dimensional existence while remaining in the dimension you are presently in. This is how, one person at a time, from heart to heart, you will create together a fifth dimensional reality, and transform the third dimension forever. This is how you will create on the surface the paradise we have created in Telos. The energies of the old paradigm no longer support you or anyone else. You must be willing to release them from your consciousness, from your old way of thinking and from your way of doing things.

Aurelia - *What am I supposed to change?*

Adama - Change the energies of judgment, the energies of expectation, the energies of guilt and shame. All these lower vibrational energies are part of a third dimensional existence which you no longer desire or validate; there is no right judgment or wrong judgment. There is no sentiment that supports judgment in the fifth dimension. You must begin to recognize, in your energy field, in your mind, in your thoughts, in your heart, when you are in judgment and release them to the higher realms.

It is not to say you are doing something wrong either, for this too would be a judgment. You need simply to recognize the difference in the vibration. Learn and practice to feel the difference between a third dimensional vibration and a fifth dimensional vibration.

Aurelia - *Why am I tired today?*

Adama - You are tired because you are in judgment of your dimension. Each time you feel tired, recognize that you are in a place of judgment. Know that you can transmute and transform the energy. This is the homework everyone will have to do to move into a fifth dimensional frequency. Everyone will have to let go of everything they know about third dimensional paradigm, and learn a new way of being. The leap of consciousness between the third and fifth dimension is huge for most of you. Start shifting this consciousness each day, and eventually, you will reach a new level. Literally, you have to be willing to leap your consciousness into the unknown.

Aurelia - I've been feeling pretty happy in the last few days, and I have been very careful not to be in judgment about anything or anybody. So I should not be tired.

Adama - We honor your efforts, my dear, but the true shift is more subtle than you think. Yes, in many ways happiness is also tied to judgment. When certain things come to you that make you happy and you get what you want, you judge it to be a good day. When circumstances come to you that you do not approve of, you judge it not to be such a good day or call it a bad day. In truth, your energy could be in a much higher vibration right now, if you so chose. But to do that and maintain it, you must be willing to give up everything in your thoughts, words, deeds, actions and desires that tie you to this dimension that you are so eager to move away from. These are not the physical activities of your experience we are talking about, but the emotions and thoughts that hold you in a lower vibration.

Aurelia - It is not the physical things I am doing that lower my vibration and energy?

Adama - Usually, it is not. It has to do with where you hold your energy. When you hold your energy in judgment of another or yourself, your vibration drops. When you hold your energy in expectation of a particular outcome, your energy drops. When you judge yourself in a space that this is hard work or that this is a struggle, your energy drops. Become aware of how you are creating in each moment. With each thought or emotion you create either positively or negatively. This is why it is said: "Change your thoughts to change your life." Negative thinking builds momentum and affects your outer life in 3D, and prevents you from embracing a 5D frequency.

Aurelia - I am supposed to stop thinking or feeling?

Adama - That would be good. Actually, it would be very good for you. You spend too much mental energy around what must happen, what you need to do, how you must do what you feel you have to do, etc. Your mind is constantly busy in many directions, trying to create your life in a certain way. We say to you that there is nothing that must happen and there is nothing that you need to do. This mental business is an illusion!

Aurelia - You say that there is nothing that I need to do! Then I hear that I don't have a book to finish, I don't have a trip to go on, I don't have to earn a livelihood, pay bills, or answer mail for my mission, etc.

Adama - These are choices you have made. Start perceiving all your "to do lists"—and you have many of them—rather as things you are choosing to do than things you have to do. In fact, in a fifth dimensional vibration, there is really nothing we need or have to do. It is always a choice. Until this distinction becomes apparent to you, you will remain in a third dimensional vibration. This is your journey, Aurelia: to understand the "truth of this" within yourself and to live it fully.

Aurelia - Well, we've never been taught to think that way by anyone since childhood. Not many people think that way. I need a vacation in the fifth dimension to learn your ways.

Adama - We know this. This is why we are giving you new instruction now, and in turn, you can share it with others. You are all in the same boat in the third dimension; very little emphasis has been put on what is most important for all of you to shift into a fifth dimensional consciousness. You and everyone else desiring the ascension into the light realm in the next few years have a new life to step into, new shoes to fill and new hats to wear. If you so choose, this new journey will begin to unfold in wondrous ways.

Holding on to what has happened before this moment and what will happen next keeps you in the third dimension. It is now time to open yourself to all that is possible as a new way of seeing, perceiving, doing and being. Be ready and willing to live in the now moment, without expectation, and open yourself to all the magic, majesty, ease and beauty that awaits all of you who step into the fifth dimensional way of being. Be willing to experience wonders and changes that will manifest beyond your wildest dreams. Realize with your heart and mind it will not change as long as you insist on clinging to what you have known as third dimensional life. It is a new vibration, a new way of being, to live in the fifth dimension.

These are the true protocols
for life in the fifth dimension.

Aurelia - *What you are saying to me now, and so much of what has been said before for this book, is so simple. Even Sananda tells me how simple it is. And yet, we cannot grasp it. It is too simple.*

Adama - It is so because it is the mind that complicates everything. We have repeatedly taught that true spirituality is so very simple. All the information could be contained in a small booklet. It is so simple that most of you are not willing to look at it. Those who wake up are always looking for more information, the latest news from the light realms, more channelings, more techniques, more activations, etc. We notice that a great percentage of you take this information through the mind and you do not integrate much of what you learn.

You read it once, and occasionally twice, and move on to the next book, the next channeling, and forget most of what you have read or heard as fast as you find the next thing to read or the next workshop to attend. You integrate only a small portion of all the spiritual teachings you have come in contact with. If you applied yourself to integrating what you have learned and becoming it, most of you would already be in the ascended state by now. We say that it is your mind, not your heart that wants all these things, and so many of you are feeding the mind at the expense of the heart.

Your heart knows it all, and certainly knows the simplest way to lead you in the state of consciousness that will create your spiritual freedom and ascension. Your heart knows the easy pathway, while your mind believes it is very difficult and complex. When we give you the simple teachings that will lift you into a fifth dimensional frequency, many of you don't even want to read it; it is boring to you. You say, "Oh well, Adama, we have heard this before." And yes, you have heard these simple teachings many times and you have not been interested in applying them. You are still lingering in pain and struggle in this dimension which you judge is no longer your truth.

Aurelia - Then it is the mind that we have to shut down?

Adama - The mind cannot be shut down. Humanity has a mind and it is there for a purpose. The physical body also has a mind of its own; it is part of your totality. You know that the vibration you seek comes through your heart. We cannot do this for you. We cannot give you a list of steps to follow to move yourself into this vibration completely. You must allow it, and allow it again and again, without any restriction, limitation or expectation that it must present itself to you in a particular way. You are such a strong creative force, and when you hold the expectation that it must present itself in a particular way, then nothing else can happen. Get used to allowing the God within, your Divine Essence, to direct your journey and guide you all the way home, step by step. You have all become experts at complicating your lives in painful ways. You create a structure of how you feel things must appear, and nothing can penetrate that structure. That is your great strength, but it does not serve you well beyond the third dimensional consciousness.

Aurelia - That is how we have been taught to create what we want, by deciding what we want to create, setting up our intentions about how we want it to be, and then focusing on it. That is the alchemy we have been taught.

Adama - But there is a difference between deciding what you want, finding the truth of what you want, and setting up a long list of how it must present itself. At this stage, most of you do not have the ability to differentiate between the two. You have been trapped in the paradigm of limitation for so long, you are having a hard time, shall we say, ripping yourself away from it. What we are asking you to do right now is to take one simple exercise and begin to play with it. That exercise consists of throwing away all expectation you have about how things should be, what you should have; simply throw it away, and with joy and gratitude, start creating and living your life in the now moment! Open yourself wide to receiving the desires of your heart, but without expectations of how it will present itself to you. Just allow, allow and be open to the surprise.

Aurelia - Throw away all expectation! We've been told to have expectation. Expect miracles and expect this or that, etc.

Adama - We are saying to you in this moment, throw away all expectation. The second step is to throw away all judgment. These are very big steps for you and for everyone else. Your mind has been focused on these two things much too long. They have been your saving grace, shall we say, in this incarnation. You have made deals upon deals upon deals. I will do this, if this happens. I will do that, if that happens. And again, it is not about this or that; it is all about the choices you make freely and willingly from your heart center. It is about being joyous in service and in your daily life, not because it is what you are told you need to do, but because it is what you want to do. It is not about wanting to move into a fifth dimensional vibration because you have an expectation that it will take away the suffering and pains you have had. It is about moving into a fifth dimensional vibration because it is who you are, it is your truth and your next step now.

Be aware that you will also face new challenges in the fifth dimensional vibration. As your body and your vibration purifies, there is always an ongoing evolution to meet and a new level to move into. Many of you do not yet realize that ascension does not end in the fifth dimension. This is only the beginning of a wondrous and eternal journey. Know that from then on, you will continue to ascend from one level to another, from one glory to a greater glory forever and for eternity. The ascending journey never ends. This is your nature and your birthright.

You must be willing to step out of the struggle you are in now, without expecting anything from it. Simply be willing to step out of it, and let everything else unfold for you, without expectation of what will happen or how it will happen. You are adequate to the task; you are more than adequate. You are so much more adequate than you give yourself credit for. There is nothing we can do to make you shift until you start to shift yourself.

Aurelia - You are blowing all my stacks! What I am writing now is certainly not what I had originally planned for my

*third book. When I set out to write a book on protocols for the
fifth dimension, I had accumulated quite a bit of knowledge
revealed by the ascended masters in the last 40 years. Some
of this information is difficult to find, and not many people
know about it. I set up an interesting structure to write this
great book, and not much of anything happened until now. I
did not feel any impulse from you to channel the rest of that
information and add your energies and wisdom for the book.*

Adama - Are you surprised?

Aurelia - I did not understand why it was not happening.

Adama - Know that when the energies are not in the right
vibration, we usually do not lend our support. I am glad
that you noticed and that you did not proceed with writing the book anyway, because it would have been written in
the wrong vibration. The information that you intended to
write is accurate and was disclosed by many of the ascended
masters in the past. And although those teachings still hold
the truth of the fifth dimension today, it is not the complete
picture. The information you hold was given from a perspective of the third dimension to assist the lightworkers then,
in preparation for the opening of their hearts and minds to
the understandings of higher consciousness.

There are pieces missing, and the next step is now being
released. The simple truths we now explain in this book
represent the frequency of the fifth dimension. It could not
be released before in this simple manner because humanity
was not ready to hear it. The minds of people were then,
and still are now, seeking to create very complex spiritual
pathways; it does not have value to them if it is so simple.
In order for you to be able to write about the fifth dimension in the new energy, you had to grow into the vibration
yourself, or at least come close. This is why the energies
were not present before. It is certainly a process that cannot
be skipped.

Seekers first had to be informed at the mental level, so that they could integrate a portion of it in the heart. What was released in the old vibration served the purpose extremely well. It assisted humanity to evolve its consciousness to where it is today. But now, you are in a new vibration, and it is no longer sufficient to take you and all the others all the way to a physical ascension in the energies of the former dispensations. Now it is all about the heart, because it is the heart that ascends first, and then the rest follows.

This former information that you so much cherish, my beloved, has served you well to get you where you are today. Without it, you would not be standing where you are at the present. Now you feel stalled to make it the rest of the way and you are asking for guidance. You are telling us that you don't know how to do it, aren't you?

Know that in order for you to write the protocols of the fifth dimension, you had to grow into the vibration yourself. It would be of little value for you to write about something you have not yet attained or understood for yourself. We congratulate you for the forward steps you have taken. We know that it has not been easy. Now that you have acquired this understanding, you can release yourself from this dark night of the heart. You are almost ready to fly.

Adama - **Ahnahmar wants to speak to you now.**

Ahnahmar - Greetings, my beloved, this is Ahnahmar, the love of your heart, speaking to you now. Because I know your energy so well, I understand your frustration and impatience. What has been happening so far has not worked for you, has it? You have not yet quite achieved the results you have been hoping for. You have stated so many times that your goal is your ascension and to move beyond this third dimension into another dimensional reality. Have you done it yet?

Aurelia - Not yet.

Ahnahmar - Over the last 40 years, all that you have studied about higher consciousness, all the mental baggage you have accumulated and all the exercises you have practiced have served to bring you slowly to where you are now, in the courtyard of the fifth dimension, so to speak. And now you feel you are stuck and do not know how to make it all the way to the final step. It is so simple; you simply have not yet succeeded in just "becoming it." Notice that we do not say, "doing it," because it is a state of Being.

I say to you become it all the way, become the Love that you are, and embrace the new vibration completely; let go of the old. So many teachings you have studied over the years, so many books you have read searching the magic key, so many classes and seminars you have attended, so many disciplines, meditations and activations you have submitted yourself to in the last many years, and yet, you have not quite achieved your ultimate goal, have you?

Aurelia - No.

Ahnahmar - I say to you now, come home, my beloved. There is so much waiting for you here, including my eternal love for you. Be willing to simply say, "My ascension goals have not yet been met with all the efforts I have put in for nearly all my life; so I don't want to use these methods any more. I will open myself to any new methods that you present to me." What you have learned in the past was useful in assisting the evolution of your consciousness to the level you have now reached, but it was yet in the third dimensional vibration. All your former knowledge will not serve you much in the new vibration and frequency of the fifth dimension. Why would you want to keep holding on to methods that are no longer working for you? Are you now willing to make this shift in your consciousness?

Aurelia - Because I was not aware of the other methods you say are more effective in the new energy. No one ever talked much about the simple ways you are now teaching. I focused on what I was taught.

Ahnahmar - Now we are presenting other methods. You are almost there. With a little shift in consciousness and attitude, you can make it all the way in a relatively short time. I ask you to love yourself enough to come all the way home now. It is your time, it is our time to be together again in a more conscious way. It is our time to be in divine union with one another in a sacred marriage of the soul, as two bodies, but one heart.

Aurelia - O.K., I am listening.

Ahnahmar - We have suggested that you turn over everything that is not helping you to purify and sustain yourself in a fifth dimensional vibration frequency. You recognize the difference, whether you think you do or not. In your heart, you know the difference, and it is for you to discern within yourself; we cannot do this for you.

Aurelia - You mean to turn it over to God, or to turn it over to Mary? Now you see, part of me wouldn't turn it over to God because I see this as my trash that I have accumulated over eons of time. I don't want to give God my trash.

Ahnahmar - God knows the truth of what you call "your trash" and also knows that your heart is trying to free itself from the bondage of the third dimension. God willingly takes that energy and says, "All this energy that you hold so tightly around yourself, release it to Us, we can transmute it and send it out to bless others with it. This action of releasing it, not only does it lift from you the limitations and burdens it holds, but also all that energy you are holding can be transmuted and released where it is most needed." Each time you give anything over, you do a great service to yourself and to all of us as well. As you free the energy, ask for the wisdom to learn from it, and you can be free.

Aurelia - That seems to be easy enough. I thought I only want to give God the good things.

Ahnahmar - No, and that is not for you to decide right now, because the issues you are dealing with are your expectations and your judgments. In this moment you are not the best arbiter of what is good for you and what is not. We are asking you to simply start working on the level of vibration. We want you to begin recognizing and discerning for yourself when you are in balance and your energy is not limiting you; turn over anything else. It is time for you to differentiate between your true identity and the illusion.

This state of awareness must come through your own heart recognition, not from us saying to your mind, "When you do this, you are in your truth and when you do that, you are not in your truth. Or if you do this, you are in a third dimensional vibration, and if you do that you are in a fifth dimensional vibration." This is your course in mastery, my beloved, your course in discernment and self re-discovery. Until you succeed to do this for yourself and maintain that level of vibration, you will not be able to remain in the vibration of a fifth dimensional frequency.

Perhaps you need to take out your pendulum and test things once in a while when in doubt or perhaps at first you need to come up with a specific method for yourself that allows you to have a clear validation. This is for you to devise. With each issue, you will look and say, "Is this a third dimensional vibration or is it a fifth dimensional vibration? If it is in the third dimensional vibration, I will turn it over to God and ask that the wisdom I need to learn from it be revealed. Let your God energy purify this vibration from you. Your job is to simply do this with trust and love for your healing, and to see what the results may be, without expectation.

If nothing else, it is something new that will put an end to your beating your head against the same wall over and over again. Will you try this?

Aurelia - I will most certainly try. I am longing to be with you in divine union for eternity, and I am willing to do whatever it takes to bridge the gap that is keeping us apart in consciousness and in physicality.

Ahnahmar - To do this simply because you want to be with me again is a good motive, but it should not be the only one. Now is your time to learn that you can easily and quickly embody your divinity and experience divine union, first with Self, and then with me.

As you leave Mount Shasta and travel out into the world, each person you meet will carry a different vibration. It will be for you to begin recognizing the vibration, not in judgment but in discernment, the truth of each person's vibration. Begin to perceive the beauty, not only of their individual vibrations, but the common thread that runs through them all. You must begin to make this a journey, not just for what you are doing in service, but also for what you are doing in service to yourself, for your own evolution. This trip will create a high-level course for you, my beloved, and know that I will be with you at every step, loving you and encouraging you to move forward into your final victory of ascension. Know that I am always with you. There is never a moment that we are apart.

Aurelia - Why do I still have a fear about traveling and leaving the comfort of my home?

Ahnahmar - The fear is not about the travel. The fear is about letting go of where you have been; this is simply the ego mind, which does not want to release the territory it has protected for so long. Each time you take a journey, there is much to be discovered. So far, in spite of the initial fears, you have enjoyed all your journeys, haven't you? And you have met numerous people with whom you have developed very significant heart connections. That would never have happened if you had stayed home, would it?

Aurelia - Yes, I have. They have all been wonderful and I am most grateful for the experiences, but I still feel quite nervous before I leave. I dread the plane rides. I think I should have at my disposal my own space ship to take me wherever I need to go. You have a lot of spaceships in Telos; perhaps I could borrow one, and also borrow a ship captain for the long travels. (Laugh)

Ahnahmar - With each trip, there has been so much unknown you have had to face. Your ego mind tells you that the unknown is not very safe, the unknown is a scary thing that can hurt you. But if you listen to your heart, it tells you that the unknown is a wondrous thing; it holds limitless possibilities of so many things you have desired. It is for you to make a conscious choice that you wish to follow your heart into the unknown, and into all the magic that these travels enrich your life with. Thank the ego mind for its concern, but simply tell it to step aside, or else turn the ego mind, in that moment, over to God. Do not debate with it because that is its territory. Simply turn it over and move back into the heart vibration that supports you on your journey. You have chosen to make the journey. Why would you not support yourself in a way that is comforting, strengthening and enlivening? Why would you continue to support yourself in a way that tires you or causes havoc with your system?

Aurelia - I suppose I don't understand how that works.

Ahnahmar - We are explaining that to you.

Aurelia - This is why I am listening.

Ahnahmar - Begin to practice it. You cannot sit down at the piano and play the sonata without prior practice, you must learn it note by note. From that learning comes your power and the return of all the gifts of the goddess that you are. Each note is a new tone for you to learn on this journey, and then, the whole set of tones comes together to sing the song to you. You are playing, now, tones from every lifetime you have ever lived in incarnation on this planet. And each of these tones, when it comes back through clear and strong, will present to you another piece of your divinity. At the end of this, you will own yourself again. It cannot be done for you, because you would not own it otherwise. You must want this with every fiber of your being, so much that you are willing to release everything you know and have learned so far that no longer serves you. Be willing to step into the unknown now, where all you ever wanted awaits you.

Aurelia - What about things like my home, my cat and my business? Do I release them too?

Ahnahmar - No, you can live your life. What you are releasing is the energy of limitation that you insist on holding. You want to release the energy that keeps you glued to third dimensional vibration.

Aurelia - I am not totally aware of how it works.

Ahnahmar - But you are. You spend a great deal of time planning and saying: "Well, I can do this when I can move there. I can do that when this happens." Surrender all thinking that is not for your highest good. In the moment, all you need to know is who you are. You need to be able to discern the difference between your vibration and the vibration around you.

Aurelia - No more planning?

Ahnahmar - You can certainly make plans, but don't hold any attachment to them. If it feels in the moment that this is your choice, then go with your choice, but recognize that in the next moment you may make a different choice. It is for you to begin to play with creative energies and to recognize that when you truly ask for something from the universe, step out of your own way, and simply allow! Stepping out of your own way means letting go of the expectation of what is to come and how it should look. Wait in joy and gratitude for the surprises. You know, in our realm, we love surprises! It frees you of a great burden because it makes what you want that much clearer, and so you have fewer choices to make.

Aurelia - I did not realize I had so much expectation.

Ahnahmar - Is this really the truth that you are feeling? Your expectations are so numerous, my dear, they have been listed in the light realm on reams and reams of paper!

Aurelia - (Giggle) Come on...you exaggerate!

Ahnahmar - Oh yes, we hear you say, "The fifth dimension will look like this, in the fifth dimension this will happen, I will be able to know and have access to all knowledge, and I will be able to teleport and to fly, I am planning a very long vacation, I will be able to ..." Endless list of expectations! Know that the way you say or do things is often very amusing and funny to us.

Aurelia - I know these statements to be true but I don't see anything wrong with having these kinds of expectations. Besides, I am trying to understand it. It doesn't mean it is expectation.

Ahnahmar - What you have perceived as "trying to understand" has been your mind trying to create a set of expectations. "If I can understand what this is supposed to be, then I can hold the image of it, and I can move myself towards it." But this is not what you are doing. What you need is to move yourself into a vibration that is already present, and once within that vibration, merge with it and then allow. When you fully understand and own it, you will desire to choose differently.

When your full consciousness is restored, you will have a much different sense of what you want for yourself and for this planet than you have now. You are now moving deeper and deeper into your own Divine Essence. What is not real are the things that are external to you. So why hold an expectation for the home you want to live in, or the people you wish to be around you, or the way you wish the world to look? It has nothing to do with you. The vibration that you seek and wish for lies within you and nowhere else. You know that.

Until you can release all that is external to you, all that is not within the Self and the truth of your divinity, you will not live in the vibration you wish to move into. It does not matter what takes place from this moment forward in your external world; it simply does not matter any more. Release all attachment to what should or can be. Can you accept this?

Aurelia - I will try.

Ahnahmar - This is not to say that you do not need to be involved in it. You will want to be even more involved than before, because when you realize that it does not matter and you are not holding any expectation or judgment, you are finally fully alive. Your own energies are finally available to you, the energies which hold the vibration you are seeking everywhere but within yourself. Within self is the only place you can seek the true union with all that exists. Once you have attained that union, everything you ever desired will be added unto you. There will never again be a need to look elsewhere. I love you more than you can possibly conceive at this time.

73

Aurelia, talking to Ahnahmar - Before we stop this sharing, there is one more thing I want to discuss with you regarding my travels. It concerns me because my energy field is greatly affected. French people all over the world, and I am told people of Latin origin as well, have similar traditions, automatically hugging and kissing people they meet, even when they meet them for the first time. They do this naturally and lovingly, but without asking if this is comfortable for the other. I am now going to Spain for several weeks, and I am not sure what to expect. Many people feel they do not need to ask permission to grab you to hug you and exchange kisses and heart chakra energies with them. They feel it is a gesture of love and acceptance, but for me it feels more like an invasion and imposition on my energy fields.

In France, in some areas, when people meet, it is the tradition to kiss everyone four times, two times on each cheek, and they insist on doing it whether you appreciate this kind of greeting or not. This practice has nothing to do with love, and it feels like bird pecking, an acquired human habit that feels very strange to me. I don't relate to this custom. In the USA, it is not the common practice; we usually shake hands with a smile while looking into each other's eyes. It is also expected by them for others to respond positively to this pecking; if they don't, they get offended or feel rejected. Those who kiss and hug as a greeting are not aware of how this exchange of energies can affect others. I am very sensitive to this energetic exchange and it is uncomfortable for me.

Meeting one or two individuals at a time is not a problem. But when meeting dozens or hundreds of people all at once when I do conferences and workshops, it really affects my level of well being. It is especially disturbing when those who still smoke nicotine come close to me; I feel the nicotine entities pulling the energy right out of my lungs, and my lungs start hurting. My lungs are particularly sensitive because I come from a family with a history of tuberculosis, and I have suffered from pneumonia and bronchitis several times. I don't want to offend anyone, but I cannot allow myself to become weakened with these practices to the extent of becoming sick. That is what happens when I travel outside the USA.

If I withdraw or let them know that this is not comfortable for me, they act offended. I am going for several weeks, and I will be meeting thousands of people. There will be those who try to hug and kiss me because they have an appreciation for what I do, and it is an accepted behavior in their culture. Each time, I feel my energy sucked right out of me. I feel drained when meeting so many people in succession, because I do not have time to recharge. Then when I return home, I am sick and it takes me weeks to recover my life force. How should I handle this without offending anyone? I feel we can love each other deeply without the habit of always siphoning each other's energies.

Ahnahmar - I will turn this question over to Adama.

Adama - I am grateful that you are asking that question so directly, because people need to know and understand this protocol. It all has to do with the honoring of your own energies and the energies of others. We have noticed how much distress this cultural habit of the many people you meet has caused to your physical body when you travel, and we support you fully in this. This is also a fifth dimensional protocol, of a different nature, but an important one.

People need to comprehend that it is not always appropriate to touch someone they do not have an established heart connection with, or do not know well, without first asking for their permission, no matter how good the intention may be. Ultimately, no matter how pure the intentions are, people always take more than they are able to give; it is the nature of this exchange, and there is nothing you can do, except avoid it. It is rarely done on a conscious level. We are not talking about relationships with partners and children or close family members.

For everyone desiring to move into a fifth dimensional vibration, you need to be willing to let go of all your third dimensional cultural traditions and habits that will not support you in the dimension you are seeking. In our culture, we greet each other with a gesture of friendship by bringing the palms of our hands together and touching the area of our heart chakra, and through the eyes, connecting with that person heart to heart by a very gentle bowing of the head and a smile. We do not always need to say anything aloud; the words can be as simple as a telepathic message such as, "May peace be with you," or something similar. The love and acceptance are sent to each other and received through the heart.

This is all that is needed to demonstrate our love and honoring of the other person(s) we meet. We consider it a great honor to be allowed to touch someone in our dimension other than family members, and we do not do this very often. It is done only when there is a special reason to do so, and 'always' with permission. This is the way it is done in our dimension and in most galactic civilizations as well. We have no need to touch each other like you do in your dimension.

This is also what you need to embrace if you wish to move into higher vibration. We are not trying to change your cultures or traditions. We are only trying to make you aware that there is a higher way, and you are free to embrace it or not. We are asking all of you, from now on, to honor those who no longer want to engage in those practices in order to maintain their spiritual vibration and energy at a level that is comfortable for them.

It is your neediness and your lack of self-love that drive you to always want to make this exchange of each other's energies. It has nothing to do with love; it has simply become a cultural habit. There are those who, consciously or unconsciously, go from one person to another for hugs and kisses. In fact, they often have a serious need for the energy of others, as they are not generating their own from within the Self. To compensate for their own lack, they are sucking energies from all those they touch. They do this in the name of love, and we say to you it has nothing to do with love. It is the ego that is needy for some affection because often, it has very little self-love.

When you hug someone, there is a mixing of energies from the heart chakra of both parties. It is not always wise to allow the exchange of these energies, especially with people you do not know very well. Very often this is how "entities" that you call "hitchhikers" from lower realms can be transmitted. This happens very frequently, my friends. We constantly see people in great distress after a gathering, when they have allowed many people to get close to their heart chakra, and energies that are not desirable to them have jumped over into their auric field. Often, it has been the initial cause of a sudden mental illness in some people who were completely normal before.

Learn to guard and protect the integrity of your own energy. This is vital to build your immortality. You are all responsible for managing your energy field in a mature way.

These people usually do not know what happened to them, and often, they go on living for years with the distress and discomfort of the hitchhiker they picked up a long time ago. I say to you that all of you who want to move into a fifth dimensional frequency can no longer afford to engage lightly in those kinds of exchanges. We do not like to talk about this subject in this book, but we feel it is necessary for you in your dimension to become fully aware of how your energies can be lost or misused. In our dimension, that kind of situation would not manifest, but we always remain in full honoring of our energies and the energies of others. This is one factor that keeps our immortality intact.

Once you learn to give to yourself all the love that is inside you from the God Essence of your being, loving yourself until that love so overflows in your heart, you will no longer need to maintain these cultural practices. They are born out of a need, and we feel that you no longer need to express them this way. It is your choice.

It is not to say that there is something very wrong with these practices, but we say that this tradition is purely a third dimensional behavior that has served you well in the past; but in the new energy, it will not. If you want to move into a higher vibration, you need to start practicing the behaviors that are acceptable in the dimension you seek to enter into. For those wishing to stay in 3D vibration, it is your choice to continue to do the things that keep you attached to this dimension.

No matter how loving and well-meaning those exchanges are, one person gains in energy while another loses energy. It cannot be avoided unless you both have the same level of spiritual energy. You don't always know this when you meet someone new or even someone you already know, do you?

It is time for you, Aurelia, to stand up for yourself and give this important teaching to the people you meet when you perceive they need to have this wisdom as part of their mastery. You are all masters in training at various levels, and if you wish to come into your full mastery, it is imperative that you start acting like masters now. If you want to graduate from this Earth curriculum you cannot continue to act in the old vibration.

For channels:
I want to make another point for our readers. When someone channels beings from the higher realms, there is quite

a multidimensional activity going on in the chakra of the channel before and after the channeling. Holding the energies of an ascended being can be challenging for a person, especially if the vibration is kept for a long time. Consider that one hour of channeling easily represents on the physical plane the equivalent of a moderately strenuous ten hours of physical work.

The multidimensional activity that is created is a gift to self for the channel, but most of the time this energy is dissipated by the channel before it can be integrated. Once it is gone, it cannot be retrieved. Most channels do not know this, and rarely after a channeling session do they allow themselves to take quiet time for themselves to integrate these energies. They usually socialize with the people they have channeled for, and the wondrous energies that were available to them are lost.

It is NOT appropriate for the audience, no matter how small or large the group is, to touch or hug the channel right before or after a channeling activity. We would like to suggest that the channel should not be touched for a minimum of two hours before and after a channeling session. Ideally, it should be longer, and quiet time is important immediately after. We realize that it is not always easy for a channel to withdraw completely from the crowd after an event, but we give you the protocol that is energetically the most beneficial.

For those receiving the channeling, the more quiet time you spend after a transmission to integrate the energies you have just received, the more benefit and transformation you receive from the channeling. The more you engage yourself in mundane activities immediately after, interacting with others and dissipating the energy you have just received, the less impact the channeling will have on you. We, the masters of the light realm, do not bring you our messages simply to entertain you momentarily. We are not interested in that. The purpose of our transmissions is to assist you in moving forward in your evolution and meeting your spiritual goals.

There are those who for years have gone from channeling to channeling, to constantly hear something new, but without integrating any of the wisdom they have already received. Often, they are the ones who complain that the channel did not say anything they did not already know. To those we say,

> *"It is literally impossible to always tell you something you do not already know with your mind, because everything that is known is already recorded inside of you. But the heart can always receive it at higher levels of understanding."*

Any transmission of light from any ascended being is meant to be integrated through the heart; otherwise it will be of no benefit to you. The mind can only hear it, but cannot integrate it.

The question we would like to ask is this: What have you done with all the information you have already received? Why have you not made much progress on your pathway, or why are you not ascended yet? Do you not know that the spoken words are not so important to us as the energy and codes of light that are transferred to you with each transmission via channeling? Do you not realize that when you choose to place yourself in the energy of a channeled transmission, you become spiritually responsible for what you receive and what you choose to do with it?

In your dimension there is a saying that "Ignorance is bliss." Though this saying is erroneous and has no validity within the soul, we would like to point out that receiving the light codes and ignoring them is a greater failure on your part than not receiving them at all. When you position yourself to receive these energies, you are also receiving the karmic responsibility that goes with them.

It is with great love and honoring that we share this wisdom and truth with you today. We long for your return with us in full consciousness. I, Adama, am ready to share with you all the keys of wisdom that you need to know and understand in the great adventure of personal and planetary ascension. In Telos, we all send you our love and support on your journey "home." And so be it.

Part Two

Various Channelings

To "lift the veil" the mind
Must open to all possibilities.
To "know" the secrets that exist
On the other side of the veil,
One must experience through
The vibration of the heart.
One must simply listen
To the frequency that exists
Within all of us,
Throughout every instant of creation.
- Celestia

Chapter Five

The Great Ship of Mu and of Lemuria

Dialogue between Adama and Aurelia

Adama - Greetings, my beloved, I perceive that you are seeking an answer to a question that is creating a very deep longing in your heart. How can I best help you today?

Aurelia - What is the difference between Lemuria and Mu, or are they the same thing?

Adama - There is some confusion on your planet and in many writings on the difference between Lemuria and Mu. Lemuria was the great continent that was considered the "Motherland" on a planet that perished in its third dimensional aspect 12,000 years ago. The land of Mu exists in another universe called the Dahl universe, and is the land the original Lemurians came from over 4,500,000 years ago. The name Mu was also given to the huge spaceship in which the Lemurians traveled from their Motherland when they first came from the Dahl Universe. The original "land of Mu" basically resides very close to the place that you know as the constellation of Cassiopeia. During the time of Lemuria and even earlier, millions of years ago, there were several civilizations that came to inhabit this planet, but they were not very enlightened about the Light that we know today, and most of them did not embody the true Christic consciousness.

On the original continent of Mu in the Dahl universe, we had built a huge spaceship that you would call today a mothership; we called it the "Great Ship of Mu" because it was at the time one of the largest that existed anywhere. At the request of the Creator, one day a very long time ago, a whole group of us embarked on a journey to your planet Earth. We left our homeland and began our great adventure towards this planet. We circled the Earth for quite some time in our ship, observing this beautiful blue planet and the people who already lived here, before deciding to step onto the soil of this land and make it our home.

Many of the beings who originally ventured out from the ship of Mu are some of the beloved ascended masters you know well today, and who, with great love, persist in guiding you "back home" to the "Heart of Mu," the place of Love and Compassion and paradise you now so long to reconnect with.

It might also surprise you to know that the captain of this great ship, in whose command the ship was entrusted, was none other than your Most Radiant and Beloved Sananda, also known in his last incarnation as the master Jesus 2,000 years ago. The master Maitreya, the planetary Christ, Masters Saint Germain, El Morya, Mother Mary, Mary Magdalene, Nada, Aurelia, myself as Adama, Lord Lanto and Serapis Bey, to name just a few, were also among those first Lemurians to set foot on this soil with the intention to bring our love, knowledge and wisdom to assist the evolution of this planet, and to fulfill the request of the Creator.

What we brought with us was the pure original teachings of Creator Source, and with this, we eventually created three long golden ages of such magnificence not imagined or comprehended in your present state of consciousness. These memories are still stored in the cellular structures of your bodies and in the infinite chambers of your hearts. With a little more patience, these wondrous memories of your former level of consciousness will begin to surface from your awareness, as you choose it, as you are willing to do your inner work and start living again from the Sacred Heart of your beingness. With our help and with the help of so many beings from this and other universes, you will be able to recreate what has always been your birthright as divine beings.

The continent of Lemuria existed as a land before we arrived, and there were very few people who inhabited it at the time, but it wasn't named as such. Actually, it had no specific name, as language was not so well developed then, and we called it Lemuria, in memory of our beloved home planet "Lemur."

This is why I, as Adama, am known as the Father of Humanity, because we were the first ones to bring forth a new race of enlightened beings on this planet. In this regard, Lemuria became an extension of the land of Mu in the Dahl universe, because we are genetically the same people. The Great Ship of Mu eventually became outdated, and was upgraded, rebuilt bigger and better if you will, at a later time with our modern galactic state-of-the-art technology. Now what you may occasionally see in the sky as the Ship of Mu is a new version of the original one.

Aurelia - This is so fascinating! I had no idea there was such a ship. Once in a while I see a huge mothership over the mountain or close by. That ship is so big that it makes Mount Shasta and all the surrounding look rather small in comparison. Each time I see that particular ship, I immediately become filled with an intense sadness and nostalgia that surrounds my whole being. I have to stop what I am doing and go hide somewhere to have a good cry and release a flood of tears. At times, I have cried for hours just seeing that ship at a distance. Adama, is this the ship of Mu, and why do I have such a reaction to seeing it?

Adama - Yes, beloved of my heart, it is; and this Great Ship of Mu is your ship. It is not your ship alone, but you were among the first ones who came with me to the Earth in that huge ship, along with other masters that you know, to give birth to the new Lemurian race on this planet. The original Adama and Aurelia *(the ancestors of our direct lineage)* who first gave birth to the new Lemurian race went back to the land of Mu in the Dahl universe a very long time ago, but you and I have remained their direct soul extensions on this planet. We are their soul progeny. We are the ones, along with several other masters, who have been entrusted with the guardianship of the Lemurian race, as well as overseeing the evolution of this race into completion and ascension. As you well know, the time for ascension has finally come. The great experimental cycle is soon coming to an end, and the planet is now ascending back to Her original beauty and perfection.

You have always wondered why you are still incarnated here when you feel that you should have ascended a long time ago. Let me tell you that many aspects of your being-ness which have lived this long dark night, since the fall of Lemuria, have already ascended. And it is only one aspect of you that is still here on the surface bringing forth the Lemurian teachings once again.

A long time ago, you willingly chose to accompany the "children of Lemuria" in their descent into darkness and to be present with them during that long dark night. This you have done very well throughout the ages; we are so very grateful for all you have done in the past and for what you are doing now. You made an inner commitment to the Creator that you would stay "with the children" in their di-mension until the very end of their experience, and see them all return home, one by one. This was your act of sacrifice.

This is why you are still embodied on the surface and doing the work you are now doing. It was a contract you willingly signed eons ago, and you did this out of love. No one, not you, not even the Creator, knew to what depth this darkness and separation would take an entire civilization. The kind of darkness that was eventually created here had not been experienced anywhere in any universe at the time. As we said, it was a great experiment. You know, and we all know, how painful and devastating this has been for you, and that you have often regretted making that decision. But it was a wise decision to make at the time, and your great sacrifice, lifetime after lifetime, did eventually bear fruit. Soon, my beloved, you will return back home with us in the arms of love, and your tears will be no more. You will be loved and cherished for eternity. The grand reception we are planning for you is not so far away as you may think.

Remember the times when you have seen the huge mother ship hovering above and beyond the mountain, so huge, and you started to cry, wondering what it represented? This is your ship, my beloved, and you were connecting with that energy. You contemplated that ship many times crying your heart out without knowing why. Well, it is the great ship of Mu; the beings there, your ancestors, find you where you are, and they stand beaming their love unto you. That's why your heart has been so deeply touched so many times by that sight.

When our ancestors come to Mount Shasta in their great ship to visit us, their progeny, know that you are not left out. In your light body, while you sleep, you are invited onto the ship to spend time with your Family of Light whom you love and miss so much. They usually stay a few days. It is often your beloved Ahnahmar or I who come to get you to bring you aboard. You receive all the Love that you are not receiving on the surface. Your ancestors love you so very deeply and are so grateful for what you are doing. You have a wondrous and happy time with them when they visit. Of course, when you see the ship again the next day from your third dimensional perspective, you do not remember anything of your nocturnal adventure, but the soul does and so the emotions surface. We all know of your reluctance to leave your family and return to your body in the morning. It is this longing for home that brings such a flood of tears.

When you first came to the Earth, we came together. You did not come as Louise Jones, of course, but as Aurelia, the original one; you were a whole being. Through the incarnations we all have experienced on the Earth, souls have divided and subdivided into complex multi-dimensional multi-personalities, all belonging to the same being. Of all the various aspects of "you," you are the one who has chosen to stay until the very end to help bring the children of Mu back home. Throughout your incarnations, you have been persecuted again and again for the Light of Lemuria that you carry, and this is why life has been so difficult and painful for you on the surface. This is why you experience pain and nostalgia when you see our mother ship. Deep within your heart, you know you are going to return there. We are all going to return together, and know that even if you are not conscious of it in your outer awareness, you often travel home in that ship with your family for short periods of time. Much wisdom and understanding will soon come to light, and eventually you will be able to visit at will as often as you wish in full conscious remembrance.

Aurelia - What is the connection between the Ship of Mu and the one known as the Star of Bethlehem?

*Adama - The Star of Bethlehem is another name for the great Ship of Mu. The Master Jesus, whom you know now as Sananda, also came from Mu as the captain of that ship. When he came to Earth on his final earthly mission 2,000 years ago, it was the Ship of Mu that appeared as the bright star in the sky then named "The Star of Bethlehem." It is again often seen in the proximity of Earth. It spends long periods of time around Mount Shasta, but it is not always there. Now, because of the Earth changes and the preparations for planetary ascension, the Ship of Mu is seen more often. The beings on that ship are the Elders, the Ancients, and they are aspects of you that are whole, as you are also aspects of them. Your ancestors consider all of you as their children and they hold great love for you. They are here to assist and to nurture you in ways that are not tangible to you yet. Nevertheless, they are presently doing much work in reconnecting with their progeny on the inner planes. It is awesome to behold.

Aurelia - What about other ships in the clouds we see around the mountain. Where are they from?

*Adama - Not all clouds are hosting ships of light. Mount Shasta is constantly visited by thousands of ships from all over the multi-universes. They do not all surround themselves in lenticular clouds. They are fifth dimensional ships of light and they are basically totally invisible to your present field of vision. This is why you see only the few who choose to be seen.

There are beings from all kinds of civilizations who come to the mountain, and occasionally they clothe themselves with lenticular clouds to signal their presence to you. They take the humidity from the atmosphere to create clouds for your benefit and enjoyment. It is their way of making themselves somewhat visible to you, and they know how delighted you are when you see those clouds. They do this to give you the sense of home as they beam their love to you. They are amused and joyful when you see their ships and in excitement you open your heart. In return, they also open their hearts to you. It always delights them to experience your reactions and your affection.

Aurelia - This is quite enlightening, Adama, thank you for that sharing. Going back to Lemuria, what actually happened to that ship when the physical, third dimensional Lemuria was destroyed?

Adama - The ship watched the destruction of the continent from space, and then went back home to its own land. Before leaving, your ancestors assisted, along with many other star brothers, lifting Lemuria into the fourth dimension as its third dimensional aspect was destroyed. They continued to support and comfort us in the aftermath, as well as assisting us in beginning to create the reality we now live in.

I want you to understand that the original beings who came in the Ship of Mu, your ancestors, are also "you," aspects of you, as you are aspects of them. Know that you are a very ancient being, a very significant one. I know you don't see yourself as equal to these ancient beings, and I say to you that you need to heal that belief because you are very equal to them. You are the one who has had the courage to stay behind, voluntarily, on the surface so very long, through the long dark night. Though you have known darkness and limitations of all sorts, it does not mean that you are "less" than they are. Temporary veils are creating this illusion of separation; that is all. Very soon, my beloved, we will all unite together in a great reunion of love, joy and ecstasy, and you will be included. We are longing for this as much as you are.

Aurelia - Adama, it feels as if part of that is already true for me on a very deep, though not outwardly conscious, level. I feel that in stages, that union and reunion is beginning to happen for each one of us.

Adama - It is, but in your outer world you haven't seen much change, have you? On the inner planes, the ascension has already taken place in many ways. It is not full ascension, but ascension one day at a time and one step at a time, gaining more wisdom and mastery with each step. There will come a time when everything, including your conscious level, the aspect of you that feels the limitations of the third dimension right now, that feels frustrated because of the veil, will lift. You will know then the glory of the inner world in your present incarnation. There will never again be any more veils. You have all created these veils on the Earth to serve evolution, and there is nothing you would consider negative about this experience.

Consider it a very long experiment that taught not only the people of the Earth, but those of many universes, galaxies and solar systems, how dense matter could become and how to bring light into matter. You are considered the brave and the courageous ones; be assured that you will receive your rewards. Hold on a little longer and continue to feel the longing for your freedom. You know the longing is healthy. It helps you walk forward and onward.

For those who will read these pages, know that this information about Aurelia is not only about her, because we are all part of a huge family. All of you and all of us carry the same seed of the Creator Light that came to Earth as Lemurians, and later on also as Atlanteans. Now, together, we are creating a new Earth and a new way of being in love and unity on this planet. The lessons learned are creating a new consciousness that will reward every effort, every pain, every sorrow and every tear with its pot of gold.

Let the diamond of your heart shine brighter each day, as you are all the stars of this great cosmic evolutionary experience, and we are already setting up the great ceremony of your graduation. Because of this, you are loved in ways that you cannot yet imagine. May our peace and great love be with each one of you, blessing and loving you each step of the way back home to the consciousness of "Mu," the consciousness of the eternal Love of the Creator!

The child of innocence you once embodied
Is now longing to play again.
Though in our realm,
We are responsible mature beings and
Always in the service of the Creator,
There is always an aspect of us
That maintains a playful nature.
- Antharus

Chapter Six

The Magic You Once Knew!

Antharus, the Blue Dragon Speaks

Antharus - Greetings, my beloved, I am so happy to reconnect with you heart to heart. It is really time for us to have our little chat for your book, isn't it?

Aurelia - Yes, and I am so happy to do this again with you. You know, our first little talk published in Telos - Volume 2 made you famous. You are now known in many countries of the world. You won the hearts of so many, and our little talk became one of the favorite chapters in Volume 2. You have become almost as popular as Adama with that one little chapter! (Laugh!)

Antharus - I rejoice that our little talk has brought back so much hope for a more magical future in the heart of so many. I know that almost everyone who has read that chapter has really enjoyed it. The goal was to bring back into their consciousness a feeling of the magic that once was so real and so natural as a way of life for all of humanity, before the fall in consciousness.

You know very well that in our dimension, there is no such thing as competition of any kind. Everyone rejoices with the success of everyone else, and because we do not live in the consciousness of duality, there is no such thing as better or worse than. We never compare levels of popularity under any circumstances. In our state of Oneness, we thrive in the beauty and joy of what is. In your dimension, duality, the spirit of competition and judgment such as "better or less than," have brought to all of you great suffering over the eons of time. This has never served any enlightened purpose; it only kept you in separation and pain. It is time for all of you to again embrace the spirit of Oneness and let go of the duality and drama completely, a true 100%.

Aurelia - Yes, I miss that magic. I am fed up with separation and limitation. I miss being able to manifest the life of ease and grace that ascended civilizations enjoy, I long for the full return of my spiritual gifts. My goal is to walk the Earth once again in the full magnificence, innocence and beauty of my Godhood. I know this is coming for me. This is the reason for this incarnation, to balance and heal the thousands of incarnations I have had here for so very long. I yearn to come home to the land of love and light where the only kinds of tears that exist are tears of pure joy and ecstasy. My whole being is longing for home.

Antharus - How can I help you today or how can I help you dream more magic into your life? You know, conscious dreaming and the right use of the imagination are the first steps in manifestation.

Aurelia - I want to fly again on the wings of a dragon, your wings, if I may. I want to cross the oceans on the back of a winged horse, like Pegasus. I also want to explore all the magical kingdoms on the back of a unicorn and dance with the fairies and the gnomes in the magical forests. I also want to play with the lions and the tigers and gently pull their whiskers.

*Antharus - My dear, your inner child, the child of innocence you once embodied, is now longing to play again. This is a good sign. It shows that you are now more ready than ever before to let go of the rigid structures of your dimension and start playing like a beloved child of the universe. Though in our realm we are responsible mature beings and always in the service of the Creator, there is always an aspect of us that maintains a playful nature. You have done all those things in the past that you are longing to do again, and you have done them for eons of time; and so have those who will read these lines.

It will surprise you to know that even as we speak, there is another aspect of you in the higher realms that delights herself in engaging and amusing herself to her heart's content in all the magical activities you have just mentioned. This is the innocent and impish child-like aspect of you that Adama and Ahnahmar love so very much, that knows only love and joy. Her time is spent in nourishing and guiding with her love the beings of a great number of magical kingdoms. Everyone has such an aspect, not just you. This is the aspect that you are longing to reconnect with more consciously. Know that you connect with this aspect very often in your dream state and often you go out at night on many great fantastic adventures.

When I mentioned using the imagination, I am not kidding. Imagination is such a wondrous doorway. It is impossible to imagine something that does not exist somewhere outside your conscious mind. It is the heart and not the mind that knows it all, and holds all the keys. It is the heart that holds those wondrous memories. The human mind, controlled by the human ego, is very quick to deny the magical side of each child of creation. If you can imagine a thing, know that you are tapping into something that already exists that you have experienced somewhere else in time and space in your many multidimensional aspects. Imagination in your world, viewed as positive or negative, is always a reconnection with some past experience held within the cellular memory.

If you are longing to do those things again, it is because

your heart is now ready to reconnect once again on a more conscious level with the aspect of you that embodies that love and pure innocence. Let me tell you even more. It is usually in Telos at night, during your sleep time, when you reconnect with that aspect of yourself. Quite often when Adama is looking for you at night, he usually finds you with the lions and tigers, the unicorns, the horses or the fairy godmothers.

Aurelia - Does it upset him to have to look for me when he wishes my presence?

Antharus - It is not only Adama who looks for you from time to time, but also your beloved Ahnahmar. They don't get upset, because they know how great your love is for those many kingdoms, and they also know how healing this is for your soul. You do spend a lot of time with them every night in your sleep time. When you get away to play with the beings of the magical kingdoms, it takes either one of them an instant to find you. In fact, they are delighted when they see you so happy.

Someday, life will be as happy on the surface as it is in Telos and in other subterranean cities. It is important that you start dreaming new lives for yourselves. Dream of new ways of being and living on this planet. Add much magic to the new lives you are dreaming about. Everything in creation always starts with a thought, then a dream of that thought and finally allowing the dream to expand into a new creation. Believe in yourselves and in your dreams and eventually, they will truly manifest in your daily lives. Have much fun dreaming and imagining; it does not cost anything and could even be quite lucrative in many unexpected ways.

Aurelia - Tell me more about how we can bring more magic into our lives.

Antharus - It has to do with reconnecting with the wondrous aspect of you that embodies the pure child of love and innocence. You all have such an aspect, but not many of you are aware of this. Even among those who are, very few have taken the time or have had the interest to consciously get acquainted with it. This aspect of you is so wondrous and so beautiful! It holds the key for you to all the magnificence of the universe, and all that you have ever wanted to be and to do. It is an aspect of you from another dimension, but an aspect that lives hidden within your Sacred Heart and awaits your awakening to its wondrous presence. This aspect waits for your readiness to allow it to be born again within you, and to create with you all the magic you once knew.

You have often abandoned this as an aspect of yourself, ignored and even forgotten about. It has always remained intimately connected to the totality of your divinity. This is the loving and playful aspect that you have scorned so often in the rigidity of your third dimension structures. This inner child is light, limitless and ecstatically joyous, and is also YOU.

In the early time of Lemuria, in the Land of Pan, you and this wondrous child were one. Life was wonderful and perfect for a very long time. There was only the magic of Love. There was not yet any separation. As you eventually allowed yourselves to fall into greater and greater separation from your Godhood and all the wonders that come with it, you gave birth to another child within, the one in pain and sorrow—the inner child that you all consciously know about, whose healing is the topic of so many books.

You gave birth to the child of the ego mind that has kept you and that child in separation and pain for thousands of years. You have caged that child in an ocean of negativity; you have neglected and abandoned that child and kept it imprisoned in fear of the many emotions that come with separation. That is the one now crying out to be healed and reunited with the child of Light who lives in so much perfection and wonder.

Allow yourselves now, from a point of choice in each moment of your lives, to love yourselves and the child of the ego mind with so much passion and compassion that all the traumas of the past will be peeled away layer by layer. The child of the ego will gradually learn that it is also a child of God and will be happy and free, and so will you. Be aware that these child aspects of you do live within your Sacred Heart and they yearn to be united by your unconditional love of all aspects of your being.

When the two unite as one, through your love of self and embracing of your divinity, by the total acceptance of who you really are as a divine being in human form, this is when you will be "home."

Like the prodigal son of your scriptures, you will be invited to return to the Father's house again. This is "when and only when" all the magic, all the wonders and all the love you once knew will be made available to you again. And it does not need to take eons of time. You will need to fully believe in yourself again and be determined to let go of all your fears and doubts.

The love and grace accorded by the Creator at this time can melt the barriers rather quickly if you ignite the fires of love in your heart with enough desire, enough passion, and enough determination and willingness to heal it all, through to completion. Know that the rewards at the end of the tunnel are the greatest love, joy and magic your present mind can possibly imagine multiplied several thousand times.

Aurelia - This is wonderful, Antharus. Thank you for this reminder. I must admit that on a conscious level, I have neglected both children of my heart. This teaching is so important, thank you. Now can you tell us more of the magic that is awaiting us in the future?

Anthaꞓus - Keep in mind that the return of magical lives you all yearn to find again can only come from divine union, your level of Oneness with all of life. In the realms of light, you simply cannot create magical lives till you become totally unified with whatever you want to create. This means when you have become the embodiment of Love and Oneness, and you radiate only Love, all of life becomes connected with you as "One." From this viewpoint, you can create anything at any time. You can have it all and do it all, whatever it is. All kingdoms unite with you as One and all elements and the nature spirits are at your command every instant to assist you in fulfilling your desires. It is their great joy and service to life.

This is, my friends, the great partnership of love and brotherhood for all.

The animals become greater playmates than you could ever imagine at this present time; the flowers and plants replenish themselves instantly and perpetually for your pleasure, the grass is always alive, but never has to be mowed. You can transport yourself anywhere, at any time, instantly. You never again have to fill out IRS reports or pay for car or house insurance. Neither do you have to deal with a nearly bankrupt bank account to pay this month's bills. Life is lavishly abundant everywhere you look. You will live in crystal palaces and never have to pay rent or make mortgage payments.

The unicorns hold the secrets to all the hidden mysteries of the many kingdoms, those known and those still unknown to you at this time, and they will delight in leading you to wondrous magical discoveries. You will wonder why you have taken so long to finally come home to the land of love and magic. This is, my friends, the life that awaits you in the fifth dimension. Nevertheless, you do not have to wait for this event to start creating for yourselves lives that are easier and more magical.

Start now and you will see how simple it can be. It is not the third dimension that limits you, but your lack of willingness to recognize that you can have now, in this present time, a very pleasant life, full of wonders. If only you believed in yourselves and opened yourselves to receiving all the gifts that life is waiting to bestow upon you. Stop denying your gifts. Your denial is the main reason why so many of you go without the gifts now waiting to be given to you. It is your denial that blocks the way.

Aurelia - What does all of this have to do with dragons?

Antharus - Those of us dragons who are beings of the fifth dimension and above hold the keys to the four elements, and we have full mastery of them. This was explained in our last message. You have heard of the magic dragons, and it is that mastery of the elements that assists us in creating magic so easily. What it has to do with us dragons, is that we would like to offer all of you reading this material our assistance in mastering the elements, so that your manifestations may come with greater ease and grace.

This is our commitment to you. We may not be allowed to interfere with your free will and learning processes, but it will be our pleasure to whisper in your ears the keys to mastery of the elements as you learn to maintain greater levels of love and harmony at all times. We offer to monitor the progress of those who ask for our assistance, though we will not be the only ones doing so. With each level of attainment you reach in your journey towards spiritual freedom through the ascension process, we commit ourselves to present the next key, and then the next one, to assist in your mastery of the element. Do you have another question?

Aurelia - Yes, there is something I want to clarify for the readers. Lord Sananda told me a while ago that because you are a dragon and a being of Light and Love I can trust you. But he also mentioned that not all the dragons and reptilians can be trusted, as there are a great many still in separation and it could be risky to trust just any dragon. He suggested that discernment must be used when encountering dragons or other reptilian beings. Can you comment on this?

Anthaius - Unfortunately this is true. Although many of us dragons and many beings of the reptilian race have reached a fifth dimensional level of evolution, not the whole race has. There are still a great number of reptilian beings incarnated as humans on your planet and many of them cannot be trusted. There are also many others functioning from the astral plane that could trick you and you must always be careful, paying attention to your feelings and using your discernment.

It is also this way with the human race. Some are ascended, radiating only Love and Light, but many on the surface are still in separation and would exploit you. Most beings in all galactic races live in the vibration of Light and Love. However, there are renegades still functioning in separation from the level of the astral plane. One must always be vigilant on your plane.

It is not likely that many dragons will come to trick you; they have other things to do. But as with any being in the universe drawn to you, some will be Masters of Light, while others may be impostors, lower level entities posing as Masters of Light. It is always wise to use your discernment and check in with your guidance. Check with the feelings sent from your heart, not those of the ego mind or from the mental level. You must do this with any being from the other side of the veil that may come to you. It is an important protection.

There are imposters mimicking each master and each group of light beings. Each ascended being that you know about must also deal with a large number of imposters from the astral plane trying to divert you or mislead you in some way from your true and most direct spiritual pathway. You cannot yet be careful enough as to what voice you are listening to. Even the best meaning people can be easily deceived by an astute astral entity. Until you have attained the maturity of your full consciousness, you always need to be careful. Not all channeled material comes from the masters of light and wisdom. The imposters are very shrewd about finding those who look for outer phenomena or those, driven by their ego mind, who are determined to become a channel before reaching the required level of initiation to be invited by a Master of Light to become their channel.

Until this planet is fully in the light, comfortably nestled in the comfort of the fifth dimension, you must always remain vigilant and use your discernment to avoid the many pitfalls of the ascension process. Those who want to deter you from your pathway and your ascension often come as impostors in the disguise of masters of light and wisdom offering teachings containing subtle and often not so subtle spiritual distortions.

Go in peace, my love, and know that I watch over you, always ready and willing to comfort you and to bring you my assistance and magic!

Chapter Seven

Message from Posid

Galatril

Greetings, and blessings to all of you gathered here today! We are blessed by your interest and your love and also by your willingness to reconnect with us again. We are here today to share our love with you and to offer guidance and support. We ask that you now open your heart to us as we open our hearts to all of you, in allowing the greatest possible opening for direct contact with us.

We have been asked today to speak about the Atlantean emergence that is gradually taking place through and together with the forthcoming Lemurian emergence in Oneness and Unity. It is with great joy and excitement that our two former civilizations are merging energies to create a new color of Love and Unity on this planet. Beware of those who will try to create in your dimension two separate emergences of our civilizations. Remember what we told you before. We, the ascended Atlantean civilization, are totally in the service of the Lemurian emergence, and we will emerge together as one heart and as one family of Light.

Our journey of exploration during the time of Atlantis will once again be understood, and we will take our place in the hierarchy of beings on this planet among the highest ranks of priests and healers, magicians and sages. My dearest brothers and sisters, know that now, after a long dark night in our evolution, we have so much love and new wisdom to share with you. We are longing to be at your side and to comfort you on your journey.

We no longer need to offer penance for our prior actions. In truth, the time we have spent working in service to the planet and humanity for the good of the whole since the fall of Atlantis far exceeds the pain and the damage we caused at the time. We give thanks with all of our beingness to the Lemurian Brotherhood of Light for assisting us unconditionally when we needed it the most. We thank them with all our hearts for their sustained love and for diligently working with us through our long period of healing.

It is now time for us to speak our truth about the time of Atlantis. It is for each one of you to perceive us in the new light we have embraced, and for all of us together to hold hands and join hearts to allow the revelations of the new Lemuria to manifest as a reality in your world.

Our time in Atlantis was the grandest demonstration of the misuse of energy that this planet and the human race had yet experienced. We were given great gifts which we chose to corrupt. We have spoken to you before about our current misgivings concerning our actions during the great age of Atlantis. In our first transmission to you, we asked for and received from all of you much forgiveness. We have released much of the denser heart energies, the pain and trauma that remained from the time of the destruction of Atlantis. We thank all of you very deeply for your compassionate heart. Your forgiveness was received by us as a gift of healing balm unto our hearts.

Those of you who lived on Atlantis before and who suffered the fall have reached into the deepest parts of yourselves to release all of the anguish and mistrust that remained from that time. Much to our delight and heartfelt relief, we see you each day continuing with this clearing and healing. As each of you cleanses the old issues and resistance that you have towards your experiences in Atlantis, we are all able to move forward to new and greater expressions of the "Heart of Lemuria."

Truly, we are now all one in our acknowledgement and acceptance of this higher dimension of love. It is now for you to bring this new dimension of love into the physicality of your dimension. Once this has taken place, our emergence together onto the planet of the Lemurian and Atlantean brotherhood will become a reality for all of us. In fact, we have been here all along with you in your dimension, but your frequency did not allow you to perceive us. Actually, it is all of you who will be emerging into the higher vibration of your own divine essence, and connecting once again with our vibration, rather than the other way around.

When that moment comes, we will all recognize each other as the true family that we are, and the labels of Lemurian or Atlantean will fall away, because we are now "one." The labels you hold regarding countries or religions will fall away. Once again we will all live together in unity and love.

Before that full emergence can take place in your dimension, many events and transformations must unfold on the surface. There are no victims in your world today. All the situations, global and personal, that you encounter in your daily life have been called into manifestation because you have created them. The greatest challenge you now face is to balance your own desires in harmony with the greater good of all. Each of you must understand completely the power of creation that you hold in each moment.

The blessings of transformation on this planet are fully manifesting through the higher vibrational energies that are increasing and also changing reality each and every day. The time of non-participation is over, and each of you is being asked to join in the great adventure. Each of you is being called to remember who you were in times past, the blessings and the pain, the joy and the sorrows. All past experiences will have their place, their wisdom and their use in your cosmic future.

In times past in Atlantis, we chose to manipulate the energies available to us for self-centered purposes. You have reached a time in the evolution of your own journey on this planet when the lessons we all learned must now come to fruition. Our hearts must continue to stay open and to embrace old and new experiences. Our minds, however, in concert with the universal mind, must recognize the truth. Atlantis became a civilization that was out of control. It became disconnected from the nurturing and compassionate energies of the heart and the soul. A great number of the Atlantean civilization became concerned with the pursuit of knowledge and power at the expense of truth. We did not honor our Divine Essence or the grace we were given.

Your world today is facing very much these same issues. Your present-day leaders are being questioned about their conduct and their motives, just as we questioned our leaders then. The answers you are receiving are not striking a harmonious chord with the music of your souls. The words your leaders speak may in some instances sound correct and the sentiments expressed may seem genuine. Yet when you examine them with the only meter that you have, your hearts, you know that you are being fed illusion, deception and treachery. You know that this illusion can no longer stand, as your Creator has decreed the "New Day of Light" for this planet.

You have all created the duality that you have come to accept and the veils that you are trying to free yourselves of. They have been created to facilitate the learning of great lessons and the gathering of wondrous experiences. Just as we created our own veils of illusion in the time of Atlantis, thinking we could play with the energies of creation and manifestation without consequences, so have you placed blinders on the effects of your own misuse of energy.

By energy, we do not only refer to the technologies that you have employed in your present civilization to enhance your lifestyles. We do not speak only of the damage that is being done to the environment of your planet, Mother Earth, and to the physical structure of the DNA in each of you. We do not speak only of the information manipulation that takes place in all of your media as a method of mind control.

We speak most importantly of the misuse of emotional energy on this planet. The emotional body is your true birthright and a great gift, and you have shut it down by denying it on a daily basis. As evolving beings of the human race, you have been gifted with an emotional body unlike any other, as were, to a lesser extent, the animal and plant life of your planet. Yet you feel the emotional body is your weakness, your "Achilles heel," so to speak. Many of you would prefer to be rid the emotional body. You feel you must contain its energy and disregard its messages to you.

The true gift of the emotional body is the ability that each of you has to experience the widest possible array of scenarios over your multitude of lifetimes, and to bring this wealth of experience back to the whole, back to all of us in the body of God. The impurity and the irrationality of the emotional body has allowed the full expression of all that you have experienced in pain and fear; and by so doing, it now allows the full expression of all that can become as Spirit. However, this concept was ignored and then forgotten. We attempted to override our emotions with the mind, forgetting that the emotions are the conduit to our hearts and souls.

You have been awarded a substantial opportunity to bring the full force of God through your emotional bodies. You are able to imbue these energies with the uniqueness that each of you possesses. This uniqueness is a direct result of the emotional coloring you have developed lifetime after lifetime in the electromagnetic and crystalline grid of this planet.

Your emotions are not energies to be ignored or subdued. They are not energies to be abandoned or mistrusted. They are truly and wholly a representation of your individual flame that must be nourished in order to burn strong and pure. The mistake made in Atlantis was to erroneously believe that we could retreat from our hearts and from all that made us human, by creating for ourselves a state of intellectual superiority which would make us more than human. This was our greatest folly, as it is for many of those in power today in your world.

The greatest gift of inhabiting a body on this planet at this time is that you are human.

You are a physical manifestation of Spirit's divine grace and potential. You are the grounding point for the expression of God's will. There is no greater joy available than when one recognizes this truth and lives it on a daily basis.

You are also expressing through your emotional bodies the connection that exists between the physical and the etheric, between body and spirit. Each time you reach out on the physical plane to touch another being, and then connect through the vibrations created within their emotional matrix, you are reuniting the realms in a new and wondrous manner. You are creating colors and energies that have never existed before, new expressions and palates of love.

Our mistake was to feel that we needed great machines and systems of energy to create in this way. We forgot our connection to each other, and competed instead to see who could control the greatest amount of energy, as if this power brought us closer to realizing our God Presence. And, of course, it could not and it did not. Only our connection to each other could do that.

Only through our love for each other could we truly touch and connect with the god within. Only through the full acceptance of our total emotional selves, in relation to one and to all, could we look again into our souls. It took our Lemurian brothers and sisters many lifetimes to show us and help us realize this truth. They supported us unceasingly with love and nurturing as we strove to release our old pictures and belief systems. They presented us with a glorious mirror of our true identity as divine beings, a mirror that we totally rejected and ridiculed in the time of Atlantis and Lemuria.

Today, we present to you this same mirror, this same love and support. Reach out to us and touch us through your emotional bodies. We are here. Feel the strength and passion for life that emerges as you reconnect with all of yourself, as you reestablish pathways and conduits for the energies that surround you. Reach out through your emotions and touch the world around you. Allow yourself to feel the trees, the flowers, the animals in the fields, the song of a bird, the flowers in your garden and the comfort of your homes. Reach out and touch each other's hearts in the most profound ways.

Together, we are creating the new Lemuria. Together, you are creating the opening that you desire for your emergence into the dimensions beyond yours. We wait for you, as we love you so dearly, keeping you always in our hearts.

Your Atlantean family is sending all of you their love and friendship!

Physical life, the solidness
That has been created in your dimension,
Is not devoid of light.
It is not darker because it is denser
Than the dimension in which we reside.
It is darker because you have lost your love for it.
- Ahnahmar

Chapter Eight

The Inner Earth City of Machu Picchu

Cusco with Adama

From the heart of the inner city of Light of Machu Picchu, from our abode of royal splendor, we send our great love and warmest acknowledgment to all of you who will be hearing or reading this transmission of Light. So many of you are indeed our former friends and family members from a distant past! On behalf of our ascended civilization here, we send our blessings to all of you, who are so diligently seeking the light of your divinity, and we bid you welcome in the midst of our energy.

My name is Cusco, and I am here at this time with our beloved brother Adama of Telos, to speak to you of our city of Light. The Peruvian city of Cusco was so named a long time ago in remembrance of my essence, for the assistance I brought to the surface dwellers of that area in past history. I am one of the ancients here, presiding on the Council of the Elders of our city.

It feels so good to my heart to be in the presence of Adama at this time. We already anticipate the joy we will experience as you read our published transmission, and we will be whispering in your ears our song of love and friendship.

Three miles beneath the outer community of Machu Picchu in Peru, a Quechua word meaning "Old Mountain," thrives another evolved civilization inhabiting a beautiful city of Light, also called Machu Picchu. Our city is similar to Telos in many ways, in the sense that our people also embody a fifth dimensional consciousness. We have been here for quite some time, almost as long as Telos has existed beneath Mount Shasta, less a couple thousand years.

Nevertheless, the history of our city is different. At one time and for eons of time parallel to the time of Lemuria, we lived above the ground, forming small communities of Light and true brotherhood, where the surface community of Machu Picchu now exists. We did not always live underground. But eventually, after the great flood and the destruction of both continents, it became obvious that the peace and the beauty we so enjoyed would eventually be compromised.

As the negativity began increasing on the surface again, darker and more violent than before, it became imperative for us to recreate our city within the Earth, like the Telosians did before us. We also desired to create a city of Light for those of the members of our Inca civilization who would eventually ascend into the higher dimensions.

We set up our intentions to preserve our culture and all its treasures underground, knowing that eventually, it could be at risk from the negativity of mankind. As the Lemurians did a few thousand years before us in building their city of Telos underground to preserve their culture and the most important treasures of Lemuria, we proceeded to do the same. Many of you still wonder where the Incas went when, at some point, whole communities disappeared from the surface of the planet almost "overnight." I now tell you that they came to the inner city of Light of Machu Picchu.

Many did not have far to go. They came inside our mountain through a secret passage in the sacred valley, not so far from where they had been living.

The Earth's civilizations have come from a wide variety of galaxies, star and planetary systems, and most of you in your long history of incarnations on this planet have chosen to experience a wide range of possibilities. You have taken embodiments more than once in all of the main civilizations that have graced the Earth through its long period of evolution.

This means that no matter where you come from originally, what planet or star system or universe, in your incarnation cycle here, you have all at some point experienced life as Lemurians, Atlanteans, Mayans, Incans, Egyptians, etc. What does it make you now? Know that in our realm, we no longer need those labels to identify ourselves. We thrive to live in the Oneness of the Creator. Everyone conceived comes ultimately from the heart of the Creator, and everyone has also left imprints and aspects of themselves everywhere in all the universes, galaxies and planetary systems.

Aurelia - *Who now inhabits your city?*

Cusco - Our inner city was inhabited at the beginning primarily by our people, the ascended Incan civilization. Eventually, some Lemurians and Atlantean scientists joined us, and little by little, more Lemurians and Atlanteans increased our number. Our city is now inhabited mainly, but not exclusively, by beings of those three civilizations. Our number has expanded much since the beginning, as more beings have joined us. Aurelia, you have several friends and former family members living here. Your family is not just in Telos; you have family in several inner cities.

We all live together in Oneness, in the spirit of total harmony and true brotherhood. You know, once you ascend, you are not limited to living in only one place. There is much freedom to move around and experience living in many places. Some people come to live here for a while and move on, and others stay for a very long time.

The way we live can very much be compared to the way of Telos. Our creation process is by thought, just as it is in Telos. Though every city has its own particulars, all ascended cultures live on the same universal principles, and the way of life is not so different from one city to the next.

The size of our city has now reached a little over one million people. What makes it different from Telos is that the inner Machu Picchu community is composed of a mix of three cultures, while in Telos the Lemurian culture is the main civilization. Many of the citizens in Telos have been alive in the same body or incarnating in the Lemurian culture for so very long, that they can almost be considered the originators of the Lemurian race. Adama is such a being and so is Ahnahmar, among many others.

As you well know, a few hundred years ago, the Spanish conquerors came to South America and ruthlessly destroyed most of the beautiful and elegant cultures living there. In their greed to acquire all the gold they could put their hands on, they respected nothing and no one. There was then a very peaceful and thriving Inca community of our people living on the surface at Machu Picchu. When the Spanish bloodshed and destruction began, we invited them to join our city, and they have not been seen since. They vacated the surface, taking their treasures with them, and moved inside. They are still here to this day, alive and well, contributing their love and creativity.

In our city, we are beings of the upper fourth, fifth and sixth dimension. As in Telos, according to their level of evolution, beings exist in several more levels and dimensions. Some of the city has physicality as you understand it, and other levels are purely etheric. Telos exists from the upper fourth dimension level of consciousness, all the way up to the tenth and twelfth dimensions.

Aurelia - What do you do and what is your main purpose?

Cusco - Actually, we are quite involved in the preservation of the "Rain Forests" which is so important for the life and welfare of the planet. Because of greed and the lack of respect and honoring of the Earth by the surface populations, without our intervention, there would be none left at this time. We are trying to stop the destruction as much as we are allowed to. Although none of us from the higher dimensions is yet allowed to perform direct intervention in your dimension, we are doing the best we can.

We are promoters of peace and harmony. We also do planetary service in our work with Nature. We have become quite adept at understanding the creation of nature, and when the time is right, we will assist the planet in restoring her original beauty and perfection. We will not be the only ones doing this; we will join the greater team. When we emerge among you in a few years, it will be our great pleasure to teach you what we have learned.

In the meantime, we make a formal invitation to all of you to come to our classes at night if you want to develop what you term "a fifth dimensional green thumb." We can teach you many of the wondrous secrets of nature that have been lost to surface knowledge that will bring much joy to your heart. In due course, you will be delighted to apply, with ease and grace, this new knowledge into your daily life to create around you the beauty and perfection of nature we have created here and that was meant to be in our dimension. In Telos, this same knowledge is used to create their outstanding surroundings.

We perform another service from our city with color. Because there is so much pollution in your world and so little oxygen left in the atmosphere, without the daily replenishing of oxygen and purifying of the air by millions of angels and ascended beings, life in your dimension would no longer be possible in most places.

As a collective, when you sleep at night, we send huge beams of a specific green light frequency into the atmosphere of the surface, purifying the air, replenishing and repairing the Earth's atmosphere. Without this, the death toll on this planet would rise over 1000 times more each day, and life would be more difficult. There are also many teams of beings from other cities of Light doing similar but slightly different work.

A great many of us contribute to your well-being by assisting the smooth functioning of the Earth and keeping humanity alive until the day of the "great cleansing," which is soon approaching. Expect it to start manifesting now through the end of this decade and beyond.

Aurelia - Do you have tunnels?

Cusco - Indeed, we have tunnels going in all directions, all over South America and beyond. We also have tunnels going directly to Telos. Actually, beings like Adama can travel between Telos and Machu Picchu in less than a couple minutes of your time. In fact, there is a whole network of underground tunnels going all over Terra.

We also have a close connection with the inner city of Quetzalcoatl at the Equator. This is a city inhabited by those of the ancient Inca and Aztec cultures. They live much the way we do and we have very heartwarming exchanges with them. Basically, we are of the same origins and culture, and in the past we have greatly assisted each other. There is a direct tunnel between the two cities.

Aurelia - Do you have a leader?

Cusco - We have leadership, yes, but not a real leader, as you understand it. We have learned to govern ourselves. We attained that level of spiritual maturity a long time ago. Of course, we have a high council like all cities do, and that is the governing board of our city. When people have reached a high enough level of evolution, the great governor of your soul and life is your Divine Presence.

Aurelia - What are your homes like?

Cusco - Most of us live in pyramidal-shaped homes made of crystal materials created with our thoughts. Many of our public buildings and teaching places are circular in shape and also made of crystal of various textures and colors. Our creativity is highly expanded and our city is very beautiful.

In Telos, it is the opposite. They live in circular homes and most of their public buildings and gathering places are pyramidal, always reflecting elegant imagining.

Thank you, Aurelia, for giving us the opportunity to express ourselves again to the many seekers of truth through your published books. We bless you with our flame of love, gratitude and harmony.

Aurelia - You are welcome. I did also have some forgiving to do regarding Atlantis, and bringing these messages from your realm is my way of showing that I have fully forgiven.

You seek to leave your physical incarnation

And ascend to another realm

Where the travails of physicality

Will not assail you.

And yet we say to you with all certainty

That all you need to transcend

Is the separation that you feel resides

Within the physical body

That you have ceased to love.

- Ahnahmar

Chapter Nine

The Effects and Uses of the Enhanced Planetary Crystal Grid

Adama

The crystal grid, or crystal life-stream as it is also known, has essentially two parts, one physical and one etheric. The primary uses of the grid relate to energy amplification *(in the physical)* and storage and transfer of information *(in the etheric)*. The grid is a direct conduit for human consciousness to access and enjoy full perceptivity in the lower Earth dimensions. Human consciousness, or mind-stream, is in truth the third grid that will be adjusted during the ascension of planet Earth.

The crystal grid has always been in place within and around the planet Earth. What you have experienced recently is an expansion of the effects of the grid in the DNA of both the planet and yourselves. This is a direct result of the ascension of the energies of the crystal grid into a higher and purer vibration. What you are experiencing today as you interact with the crystal grid in the ascension process is what the planet herself is undergoing. Through this interaction with the planet's process, your physical bodies are also restructuring. Your own crystalline structure is ascending through the adjustments of your DNA. This happens, my beloveds, as you increase and maintain your level of love and light quotient, day by day through the energies of the heart. There is really no other way.

Why is this happening? It is happening because it is now time for humanity and for the Earth to move into a much higher level of existence. It is also because you have chosen it from the level of your higher self. You have had enough of separation, and you have requested the necessary assistance to bring forth the change within yourself and on your planet. Throughout the last 20 Earth years, as measurements were taken of your willingness to move out of the denser energies in which you have resided for so long, the grids have been recalibrated for your benefit. First the magnetic grid, the geomagnetic lifestream of the planet, was adjusted. This allowed for a greater connection with the etheric realms, and dissolution of much of the veil of duality and illusion.

Then the crystal grid was raised into a higher vibration and many of you heard the call to work more actively with these energies. All of you are experiencing the vibrational shift of the grid, whether you are conscious of it or not. Your own vibrational rate is entraining itself to that of the grid, and so the planet as a whole is fully involved now in the ascension process.

To interact with the grid in a more conscious manner, you must gain a fuller understanding of its uses. You must make a commitment within your heart to access the grid only as appropriate, for the good of the whole. In times past, as witnessed in the age of Atlantis, this grid was often accessed for corrupt purposes. While the lessons learned and the experience gained was valuable beyond question, you still need to fully understand its proper use. The misuse of the grid will not be allowed to happen again. Those who might try will face a quick return of their negative energies upon themselves, and the karmic consequences of their self-centered agenda.

Since the fall of Atlantis and Lemuria, the etheric crystal grid was moved away from the atmosphere of the planet. This action was taken to protect the grid from further misuse and corruption of its matrix. The planet and humanity were allowed to live without its direct etheric influence for a long time, and this has greatly diminished your natural spiritual faculties, what you call spiritual gifts. As a result, you have lived since with less than 10% of your full potential, compared to the 100% you once enjoyed. This action was taken because it was recognized within the mind of God, and translated through the spiritual hierarchy, that the errors of Atlantis could very well be repeated. If allowed, there are still those in incarnation at this time who would very much like to recreate a similar scenario. Fortunately, their numbers are smaller than before, and very soon, they will have to transform and embrace their divinity or ship out to continue their evolution elsewhere.

We did not understand the fall at the time. We needed to understand and integrate what happened and the wisdom gained from it. We did not wish to blame or punish anyone for the events in Atlantis. In truth, all who resided there as part of that great experiment did so willingly. We honored them for the role they played in increasing our understanding of all aspects of spirit. But the extreme misuse of energies that threatened the life of the planet forced the Creator to end the evolution of that civilization prematurely. The lessons were not allowed to come to completion.

Following the fall of Atlantis, we moved the etheric crystal grid away. This disconnection created the breeding ground for new human lessons and the events of your history. Much experience was chosen, created and learned that would never have happened in the purer atmosphere of the grid. We eventually came to understand the fall of Atlantis and its contribution to the human experience of free will. Today we find a world once again poised for self-destruction, although perhaps not with such violence and devastation. This time the scenario is more like a slow and painful auto-immune disease, which eats the organism away from within.

So, my friends, we are now once again connected into the grid, both in your realm and in our own. We are all involved in a process that will lead to the eventual reopening of the heart of Lemuria. The lessons of disconnection from God have been learned and relearned, explored and examined from every angle. We have gathered all the knowledge that we can from it, and it is time to move on.

Throughout your recorded art and history, creation has been depicted as the divine spark igniting into form. This is a beautiful and powerful image that carries the full majesty and grace of the Divine. It inspires purity of emotion in those who view it, but the full properties of manifestation involve more than just inspiration. One cannot create in the physical world without the physical process of crystallization.

Crystals, and the process through which they are formed, unite both the higher and lower aspects of the Divine. It represents in that moment of inception a union between the Divine and the elementals that reside in the Earth. It also represents a downloading of information, as each crystal is a storehouse for particular energies and experiences.

Many of you have had one or several lifetimes in pure crystalline form. Many of you have imbued crystals with aspects of your greater self for the betterment and education of others who came after you. Many of you have also imbued crystals with aspects of yourselves so that you, yourself, could reunite with them later through the conduit of the crystal.

While the spirit that resides within a crystal may not appear as active as your own, it is in fact equally, if not more, expansive when directly activated by a willing spirit in human form. The seeming slower rate of vibration in some crystals is a function of eons of patient service spent embedded in one physical location for millions of years that these spirits have performed. We owe them a great debt for their willingness to remain in place, anchoring their energies until the time arrives for their release into the greater crystal matrix.

As the etheric crystal grid was once again moved closer to the planet, it awakened and reunited all the guardians of our energies which reside in physical crystal form. The physical crystal grid of this planet was reactivated with the will of the Divine. Through this physical grid the full ascension process of the Earth herself has begun, and will continue until the vibration of the planet reaches a dimensional shift and reunites with higher aspects of Her divine essence. Human consciousness will then reach a new and greater level of awareness.

At this time, you who have taken this journey with the Earth will begin to embody again your higher aspects and reunite with us. Indeed, we are these higher aspects of you. Today many crystals are ascending into higher forms of service.

This new human awareness will grow through higher information and understanding which crystals impart willingly when asked. The greatest awareness will come through opening the heart, for this is where the soul resides without judging the experiences it has collected. It balances neither trauma against pleasure, nor service against gain. It merely accepts all aspects of self as valuable and necessary to the whole.

The soul finds in the mirror of the crystal grid, both physical and etheric, the highest representation of what it wishes to live, in human form, on this planet. This too is an important aspect of the grid; it unites all energies into one flow and amplifies the life force of all that comprise it. It connects all thought and heart energies. When you access it, as do your "crystal children," you immediately become part of the greater whole.

Through the grid, you reach into the hearts and minds of all who are connected to it. You can receive the answers to all questions asked, and the healing and manifestation energies necessary for any endeavor or service you may want to initiate. You touch the higher aspects of Self and all others as well. You amplify your own divine essence both in your realm and in all others.

The proper use of the grid is essential and the proper intention for its use mandatory. We are here to work with each of you individually and often in groups on the appropriate ways to access both grids. We cannot give you generic techniques for this. You all have your own unique place in this grid, and one method alone neither works for all nor promotes the greatest awareness.

Many of you have worked with the grid before and you will find that working with it again will come to you naturally. Others will find it easier to begin to connect with individual physical crystals that live in your homes or immediate environments awaiting your attention and discovery. Practice will in time greatly improve your communication skills with crystals.

Each of you is now experiencing the restructuring of your DNA into a purer crystalline form. You are experiencing physical, emotional and mental shifts and realignments. These may appear strange, painful and uncomfortable for you, which is merely caused by your resistance to the shift. Set your intention that all shifts are for your highest good and you will remove much of the resistance. Interact actively with crystals in your healing of past traumas and release of toxic energies.

Connect with us through a crystal, or simply through your

mind, and ask for instruction on the crystal grid. Then connect with the crystal grid itself and ask for instruction. Share with others what you discover, for each of you holds a piece of this new awareness.

We bless you, love you and keep you always in our hearts. Look for us in your awareness, for *"We are also you."*

Once you evolve your consciousness

Into a state of immortality,

You will find that

All happens effortlessly.

You will find that moving on in years

Only makes you wiser,

More mature and stronger.

- Adama

Chapter Ten

The Fountain of Eternal Youth and Immortality

Adama

Aurelia - *Adama, please talk to us about the Fountain of Eternal Youth and Immortality. Are you saying that it is created by our thoughts and intentions?*

Adama - Of course, but this is only one aspect of it. *If you truly desire to attain this level of perfection and state of consciousness, you must first desire it with all your heart, mind and soul. This is your **first key.*** Around the clock, every day of your life, you must set out to renew your intention to reach that level of perfection, engaging all your spiritual faculties until you reach your goals. *Constancy is your **second key.*** On and off attempts have never brought much results. Maintaining absolute constancy in your intention and willingness to do what is required to attain that state cannot be emphasized enough.

> ### *The fountain of youth and rejuvenation you are seeking lies within you always.*

It is there, waiting for your awakening and your awareness of it. The keys to finding it have never been secrets. In fact, they have been known all along, but you have ignored them. For eons, you have been more interested in finding it through an external source, a quick fix as a substitute for true spiritual transformation. This is your *third key.* I ask you now: Have these external sources worked for you, my friends? Has your society succeeded in eliminating aging, illnesses and death? Or are you building more nursing homes, hospitals and medical clinics?

Very rarely on the surface, up to now, has any person been willing to apply the keys of transformation to bring about complete DNA transformation and immortality. Nevertheless, over the ages, there have been a few exceptions. *Your DNA is another key to your fountain of youth and infinite vitality, the fourth key.* It evolves at the speed that you evolve your consciousness and increase your love quotient. Your body is a mirror of consciousness. As it evolves, the body will begin to mirror the new consciousness you have attained. The fountain of youth has always been there inside of you, but you have to evolve your consciousness to activate it.

Your thoughts, your words and your feelings are the fifth key. What is the quality of the internal dialogue that you entertain within yourself moment by moment? Does it reflect what you desire to attain? After you have done a few minutes of affirmations each day, what thoughts do you occupy your mind with the rest of the day? How well do you monitor your thoughts, your feelings and the words you speak to yourself and to others in each now moment? How do you feel about yourself and your body?

Once you evolve your consciousness into a state of immortality, you will find that all happens effortlessly. You will find that moving on in years only makes you wiser, more mature and stronger. Yes, we become older in age, and we do it with grace, nobility and dignity as masters. It is also your destiny to reach this level of mastery. Maintain your physical prowess, agility and strength by all the means you know. You will find that the more you do, the more you will be able to do.

Don't let age or what people say limit you. You are unlimited beings who have forgotten this about yourselves..

The Fountain of Youth you are seeking is a state of Being, not so much a state of doing.

To activate this wondrous fountain, you must first unite with it and then become it. This is your **sixth key,** *and a most* important one. The true fountain of youth is a fountain of Pure Light, a fifth dimensional tool. In order to activate it within the self, you must increase the light in all the cells of your physical body as well as your more subtle bodies. You must cleanse your emotional body of negative human emotions; you must monitor your thoughts and begin to think and act like a master. If you are not sure how a master thinks in any given circumstance, go into meditation and ask that question. What would a master do, how would a master view this and what is the action a master would take? How does it feel to be a master of divine expression like our brothers and sisters in Telos? Your heart knows all the answers and always has. You only need to consult it and learn to tune in again to its wisdom.

Begin to consider your bodies as "magical forms"; see them as the most versatile machines ever created that can do all you want them to do without pain or limitation. They can even teleport anywhere in this universe, close to the speed of light, when you have attained the necessary level of consciousness. It is up to you to change the perception you have held about your bodies so far, and to learn how to utilize the full physical potential with which these vehicles are endowed.

Begin to live your new truth, and the results you are seeking will follow. It cannot be otherwise. This is the **seventh key.** In this regard, the fountain of youth is real. It is located in your very own mind and heart. You will be surprised and joyous when you discover how easy it is to maintain your youthful appearance.

The beings portraying the " dark forces "
Understand very well the principle
Of building momentum.
They are far more vigilant
In building their momentum of darkness
Than the People of Light have been
In building their momentum of Light.
- Master Saint Germain

Chapter Eleven

Assessment of Your Taxation System

Adama

Aurelia - *Adama, as children of God on this planet, is it spiritually valid and moral that we are subjected to such a controlling tax system? How do you perceive this corrupt system?*

Adama - We certainly don't have any kind of taxation system; neither would we allow such a thing. An enlightened government does not need to tax its people. Your taxation system is strictly a manipulative three-dimensional creation, spiritually immoral, demonstrating a primitive understanding of leadership and management.

We acknowledge your desires to be sovereign in this regard and your divine right to be tax-free. You are the beloved children of the most loving and wealthy Father: Source energy. Your Creator does not tax you, and neither should anyone else. Like so many other things in your society that you don't like or agree with, it exists simply because you allow it. You have given away your powers and your rights to be sovereign. As a collective, until you take your powers back, it will continue.

Be assured that within 5 to 10 years from now, and hopefully sooner, you will most likely become tax-free forever. As the Light shines on this planet brighter each passing day, your tax system will also evolve and eventually be abolished completely. There is no tax system in the fifth dimension, and if this is where so many of you are choosing to come, you will not find a single tax collector anywhere over on our side of the veil. They will remain gathered in the third dimension, wondering what happened!

We are a free and responsible society. Each and every one of us takes equal responsibility for the wise and successful economics of our society. Everything we need or use is obtained through a well-designed "barter system" ensuring an "equitable exchange." This gives us great latitude and freedom in our exchange system and makes bartering "fun," and everyone enjoys in great abundance everything they need. This is never accomplished at the expense of another, and there are never any losers.

We value our freedom above all else. We would never allow a system of taxation to exist. It would deprive us of our undeniable rights to abundance, freedom and the pursuit of happiness. On the surface, your governments have programmed you to believe that you have to pay taxes; this is a most erroneous concept. You are burdened not only with income tax, but also with sales tax, property taxes, school taxes, activity taxes, food taxes, as if eating and nourishing your body is a luxury, and hundreds of other more subtle types of taxes that are hidden or included in the price. All these taxes contribute to your stresses and burdens.

In your lives on Earth, this type of control was never meant to become part of your reality. Why do you then allow it with so much fear and complacency? Why do you then allow the leaders you elect to oppress in such a manner? And why do you still think that paying so many taxes in every aspect of your life is a normal way of sharing the meager earnings the majority of you live on?

Any government or leadership compelled to tax their people so heavily in order to function financially is a sure sign of poor administration. With a bit more enlightenment and much more integrity, your governments could function very well and with great prosperity without having to tax the people they govern. Citizens of other planets do not have to be taxed by their governments and no one lacks anything, including those doing the governing.

Aurelia - But Adama, how do we do this? Those who refuse to pay their taxes go to jail, they are harassed without end, they have their vehicles taken away from them and very often their land and their homes.

Adama - We know this, my beloved, we know this only too well, and this is all about to change in your country and gradually everywhere else in the world. This is why we do not suggest that you make waves at this time and refuse to pay your taxes. If you did that now, too many of you would be hurt. You have enough challenges in your life as it is, and we do not want to see you suffer more. The concept of becoming tax-free has to evolve first in your consciousness and then in the consciousness of the majority in order to change smoothly in an enlightened manner.

When the majority of the people in a country, let's say about 70% to 80%, have embraced a new truth for themselves as sovereign beings, and make a sincere and empowered choice from their heart that it is no longer their truth to be submitted to taxation, and call out to their Creator for his assistance in implementing this new truth, be assured it will happen and it will not take very long. But the collective has to choose it first from the heart and let go of victimhood consciousness. This is a requirement.

Know with all your heart that your sovereignty has to come first from within the self. Know with absolute knowing-ness that as divine beings, as the children of a most loving

Father/Mother, you have full rights to the bounty of this planet and of this universe which is not reserved for the few but is meant for all.

There are those in your society who have incarnated for the purpose of creating more enlightened forms of government in the near future. They are sufficient in number now to succeed and have gained enough maturity to take their place very soon. They have been trained between their incarnations to do just that, and they already know how to implement those positive changes smoothly. They are well versed on the art of leadership to implement new forms of government that will function for the benefit of all. When a governing body acts for the benefit of the collective instead of personal agendas, everyone becomes abundant and has everything they need to enjoy life. No one has to go without. Very soon, my dear children, there will no longer be the "haves" and the "have nots." Everyone will have plenty to live and function well, including all levels of government.

Be patient a little longer. Continue to evolve your consciousness and let go of the many erroneous belief systems you have been imprinted with. Those who have incarnated to implement the new forms of government will not be allowed to take their rightful place until most of you have made sufficient changes in your heart and your consciousness. It is important that you claim it and demand those changes from the heart of your Creator and from the love and compassion of your own heart. It is also important that you all continue to do this until it happens.

Remember that it is always the collective consciousness which holds the power to make decisions. Your governments can only reflect the collective consciousness of those they govern. They are mirrors, my friends, just mirrors! You all have to change first; then you will see how smoothly your governments evolve and change. It is up to you to lead the way from the fires of your heart.

Aurelia - *But Adama, 80% of the population is a large number; it will take forever for everyone to evolve their consciousness to the extent you mention.*

Adama - Not as long as you might think. I mentioned it before and many other masters have mentioned it as well. Soon on your planet, there will be events that will assist humanity to wake up and accelerate their consciousness. These events are now hanging over your head. People will have to change voluntarily or leave their incarnation. The abuse of your planet and its people by your governments will no longer be tolerated. This is what your Earth Mother is now choosing for evolution on Her body, and it will be implemented. No group of people incarnated on this planet will have the power to stop it. The shape-up or ship-out warning that was given some time ago is more valid now than ever before.

You are not alone, my beloveds; you have more support on your planet now from all over the universe than ever before. No planet has ever been given such great assistance as is granted here at this time. Be of good cheer, your deliverance is soon at hand. If only you could feel how much you are so dearly loved, your pains and worries would melt instantly into an eternal fountain of joy. We love you all so very much. Please hang on a little longer! I am with you always.

Part Three

The Sacred Flames

and Their Temples

The frequency of forgiveness
Is of the frequency of heart.
Tapping into the heart allows you
To inform the mind and the body
Of this gift,
Not just for this lifetime,
But for all lifetimes as well.
- Adama

Chapter Twelve

The Seven Flames of God for Seven Days

Adama

At this time, I want to give you a short overview of the seven major Rays, or Flames. It would be very beneficial for each one of you to focus each day on the energies of one of the seven major Rays that flood the planet from Creator Source on that day. All energies of the seven Rays flood the planet daily, but on each day of the week, one of the Rays is emphasized.

Working with the seven Rays in this manner will assist you in a most profound way, to balance these energies in each one of your seven major chakras. This will bring much greater balance and ease to your present life. In the process of ascension and enlightenment, all seven major Rays, and later on the five secret Rays, must be balanced and mastered in order to move on to greater wisdom and mastery in your cosmic future.

In Telos, we work much more effectively each day by amplifying in our hearts, our minds and our daily activities the specific energies of each day of the week. We invite you to sincerely experiment with this. You will be pleasantly surprised to discover and experience the increased energy available to you.

Sunday, the Yellow Ray of Wisdom
and the Mind of God is amplified.

Focus on the Mind of God daily in all things, but specifically on Sunday. This divine mind will open your own mind to greater and greater Wisdom. True wisdom always comes from the mind of higher perspective and higher consciousness. As you merge this divine mind with your own, you will begin to make decisions and conduct your life in ways that will bring you greater satisfaction and ease.

Monday, the Royal Blue Ray of
the Will of God is amplified.

Focus on the Will of God for your very life through total surrender to that Divine Will, no matter what your present circumstances appear to be. This is the fastest way to gain your spiritual mastery and freedom. As you align with God's Will, you will notice that your life will align in greater harmony. Bathe your mind, body and soul each day in this energy, and soon, you will reap the many benefits.

Tuesday, the Rose-Pink Ray of
Divine Love of God is amplified.

Focus on the transforming and healing influence of the energies of Divine Love. Love is the glue that creates, transforms, heals and harmonizes all things. Take time in your life to breathe it in and merge with this Flame of Divine Love. Love is the key to the power of multiplication of all good things you desire. As you merge with this Flame in a greater and greater measure, limitations start dissolving and you become the master of your destiny.

Wednesday, the Emerald Green Ray of the
Divine Flame of Healing, Precipitation
and Divine Abundance is amplified.

Focus on the energies of divine healing in all aspects of your life. This is a balancing and soothing energy that will assist you to realign the many distortions you have created in your lives. Invoke and visualize this radiant green liquid healing light for all areas of your life that need transformation. The Green Ray also governs the laws of divine abundance and prosperity. Invoke this great emerald green Flame to pave the way for the manifestation and precipitation of all your physical and spiritual desires.

Thursday, the Golden Ray of the Resurrection Flame is amplified.

Focus on the energies of this Flame for the resurrection and restoration of your inherited divinity. You are a divine being, experiencing human life, and learning from it. Because you have strayed in consciousness, your divinity has been veiled. As you invoke and merge with the purple and gold energies of the resurrection Flame, you will begin to resurrect all the gifts and attributes of your divinity. This wondrous Flame prepares you for the final ritual of ascension. Ascension has been and still is the main purpose for your many incarnations on this planet.

Friday, the Pure Dazzling White Ray of Purity of the Ascension Flame is amplified.

Ascension is the alchemical marriage or divine union of your human-self with your Divine Essence through the process of purification of all misqualification of God's energy throughout your many incarnations. Focus on purifying and clearing all negativity, false beliefs, poor attitudes and habits that do not enhance your spiritual mastery. Fill your auric field, every cell of your physical body, your mental, emotional and etheric bodies with this pure-white dazzling Ascension Flame. In your daily meditation, do this with all the Rays. It is essential for your spiritual progress.

Saturday, the Penetrating Violet Ray of Transmutation and Freedom is amplified.

On that day, focus on the many tones and frequencies of the Violet Ray. This Ray is most magical. The Violet Flame is the frequency of change, alchemy, freedom from limitation, royalty, diplomacy, and much more. As you fill your auric field and your heart with the wonders of this Violet Flame, its frequency will begin to clear the obstacles and karma that are obstructing the realization of your mastery and divinity. Use the Violet Fire as much as you can each day, but especially on Saturday when this Ray is amplified; it will serve you well.

As you see, my dear friends, all of the Rays are important. None of them can be neglected or put aside. They all work together in great harmony to assist the restoration of your soul and your lost paradise. Self-realization and God-Mastery come from the daily and diligent application of these seven Flames, as you are the "responsible" architect of your life. These immortal and eternal Flames of God will work for you as you work with them. No one can or will interfere with your free will and no one can do it for you. Spiritual progress is brought forth through daily application of God's laws, God's energies through the main seven Rays, and the clearing of one's karma and emotional body.

Each day, it is most important that you set some time aside to do your spiritual and inner work. Invoking these Flames of God's Love and Attributes opens the understanding for greater application of cosmic laws. Breathe, invoke and fill yourself with these wondrous Flames. In your meditation, seek deeper understanding of these Flames by contacting your GodSelf and your guides, and diligently apply what is shown to you. Seek to lift the veil of mortal illusions and reconnect with the magic and powers of the original intent of God for your eternal journey into greater purpose and destiny. Our assistance is available to you for the asking; a simple prayer request from your heart brings us into your forcefield instantly.

Note from Aurelia: Information on the First Ray of the Will of God and the Seventh Ray of the Violet Flame of Transmutation is included in Volume 2 of the Telos series. The Fifth Ray of Healing is in Volume 1. For even more complete discourses on the Flames, including prayers and invocations, see the book **The Seven Sacred Flames.**

Chapter Thirteen

The Illumination Flame, A Second Ray Activity

With a Meditation to the Temple of Illumination

Adama with Lord Lanto

Greetings, my beloveds, this is Adama. I am here in your presence today with several beings that most of you already know, or at least have heard of. Among those present are our brother Ahnahmar and the guardian master of the Second Ray, Lord Lanto.

Aurelia - Hello, Adama, we would like to discuss with you today the attributes and uses of the Illumination Ray to receive better understanding of this ray. You must have read our minds since you brought Lord Lanto with you. We welcome all of you in our midst and in our hearts; we are honored to have your presence with us.

Adama - Thank you, my beloveds. It is also our pleasure and honor to be sharing our love and wisdom with all of you, and later on with those who will read our published books. At this crucial time of Earth's transition into higher consciousness and dimension, it is more important than ever for every soul incarnated here to understand what is going on energetically and physically on your planet, and to advance your evolution with the new flow of energy.

Indeed, more than ever, you all need more enlightenment to fully understand and remember your divine essence, to know what you are doing here on this planet and to discover the purposes and goals you have set for your experience here. It is time now for you to take advantage of this most wondrous window of opportunity for spiritual liberation through ascension being offered to you. Because of the deep love your Creator has for each of you, and through the divine grace available to you from His Heart, you can be liberated from the choice of separation from Him that you made a long time ago.

You have been evolving here for a long time in a spiritual slumber, which has brought you much discomfort, unhappiness, pain and limitation. Through the self-imposed ignorance and separation you have chosen to experience, you have forgotten how to manifest your lives as the divine beings you truly are. Many of you have had enough of this unnatural way of being, and have called forth the intervention of your Creator. Lifetime after lifetime your souls have been imprinted with erroneous belief systems about God and about yourself. You have followed the limiting teachings of religions, whose leaders had an agenda to keep you in spiritual ignorance, control and submission. For most, these religions and dogmas you have been so attached to have kept you boxed into an endless stream of erroneous concepts, preventing you from experiencing yourself in your many incarnations through the eyes of your divinity.

We desire to talk to you of a level of spirituality whose essence is pure. True spirituality is a very simple concept and can be summarized in a small booklet. We have mentioned this several times. It is so simple that people have completely forgotten how to "be" and how to embody spirituality. You always look for the most complicated concepts you can find. Through the ages, millions of books containing very elaborate and complicated ideologies about God have been written. Actually, very few, if any, acknowledge the simple truths that pure spirituality offers. A great number of your spiritual books have been written by those whom we consider spiritually blind, desiring to guide those of humanity who are also spiritually blind. True spirituality is a state of being, a pure state of consciousness that brings you back to the true Love, true Light and true Life of your divinity.

In general, spirituality cannot be gained by the many things you do or don't do, nor by all the many rules imposed on you by your society, your religious organizations and your governments that you so eagerly conform to. It simply "IS." This is why all the rituals, practices and concepts with do's and don'ts that you accept or reject were meant only as basic guidelines by well-meaning people. These guidelines could have assisted you if you had used them from the right perspective, but they could never inject true spirituality into your soul. You alone can do this in loving communion with your divine essence.

This is why the purpose of our discourses and writings is to bring forth a teaching that is simple for people to follow, a teaching that will assist to bring you back to the consciousness of the "God within" as the great architect of your lifestream. We wish you to rediscover, as we have, the joy and bliss of living your lives according to your own unique pathway, totally connected with this divine essence that beats your heart. We wish you to remember in each moment that this divine essence is alive and active within each one of you and is the only true "Source" of all that you can be, all that you can know and all that you require to manifest your daily lives as divine beings. The river of life, of love, of limitless abundance and of every good and perfect gift you may wish to enjoy and are yearning to obtain lies within you, awaiting your recognition and your dedication in calling it forth. With this introduction, I am now going to talk about the Flame of Illumination, one of the attributes of the God-Flame that can greatly assist you in your re-awakening and your pathway to ascension.

Aurelia - Adama, what are the attributes of the Second Ray of Illumination?

Adama - The Ray of Illumination has to do mainly with God-wisdom, true knowledge and enlightenment in all its various facets. It represents Christ consciousness illumination, understanding, perception and peace from the heart of God's omniscience. It is literally an unlimited extension of the Mind of God. Many of the souls incarnating on the Ray of Illumination by divine appointment become teachers to humanity. Many of the great masters of wisdom you have heard of, who have incarnated in the past as great teachers for humanity, are beings whose main soul pathway was the Ray of Illumination. To name a few, the master Jesus/ Sananda 2,000 years ago, Lord Maitreya, Lord Buddha, Lord Confucius, Djwhal Khul, Lord Lanto, Master Kuthumi, and many others. Masters of all the Rays have also incarnated from time to time to become teachers because humanity must learn to understand and master the initiations of the Rays in perfect balance to qualify for ascension. Everyone has been created on one of the twelve Rays and there are millions of beings on each one. Understand that no one Ray is better or lesser than another, as some of you would like to believe. All of the Rays must be embodied, understood and integrated equally.

The Illumination Ray is associated with the crown chakra known as the thousand-petal lotus flame. As you invoke the Illumination Ray in your crown, the thousand petals of your crown chakra become illuminated again, expanding your reconnection with the true Mind of God, which has lain dormant within you for thousands of years. However, it has never left you, and this is what you want to awaken now. All the pockets of darkness, your sleeping consciousness, embedded within you through ignorance, prevent you from experiencing the "Mind of God" in its pure form. When you invoke the Illumination Ray in your crown chakra and in the totality of your consciousness and set your intention to re-awaken all the attributes of your divinity, your higher self will use the energies you are invoking to gradually lighten and clear the dark pockets which have been lying dormant for so long.

Aurelia - Does the Illumination Ray have an essence or a color?

Adama - The Illumination Ray is golden yellow like the sun, and quite brilliant. The "Temple of Illumination" is the main focus on this planet for this Ray. It is situated at Lake Titicaca in South America. The guardians of this Ray are the God and Goddess Meru who have held the energies of Illumination for thousands of years in that most awesome etheric temple. In Telos, we have created a smaller version of this majestic Second Ray Temple, as we have done for all the various Rays.

In the time of Lemuria we had thousands of temples on our continent representing hundreds of attributes of the Creator for every aspect of our evolution. We had over a hundred temples dedicated to the various Rays alone. You have known about seven, and now about twelve, but understand, my beloveds, there are many more. It is not necessary that you be aware of all the Rays at this time, but it is of utmost importance for those aspiring to ascend in this incarnation to gain mastery on the first seven Rays, and then later on, the next five.

Aurelia - What initiations might one go through while working with the Illumination Ray?

Adama - The initiations will involve becoming aware of all the erroneous beliefs you have entertained about yourself, that have occupied your consciousness and kept you in so much pain and limitation. It is about stepping out of ignorance and uniting with the Mind of God. As you integrate and infuse yourself with the Ray of Illumination, you invoke the Mind of God to do its perfect work to transform your own mind to new levels of evolution.

There is the human brain and there is the Mind of God, which are not the same. The Mind of God represents a universal consciousness that knows everything and holds no limitation. The human brain is governed by the human ego and is imprinted with fears, limitations and erroneous beliefs about the self. It has been altered by the human ego and its own fears, and the consciousness of separation. However, it has been a tool for your evolution, and it has served you well. Your human mind, as it evolves, is destined to unite with the Mind of God. Do not plan to get rid of it as some of you would like to do. It is yours and you must own it as an integral aspect of yourself.

You need to transform the human mind by right knowledge, true wisdom and surrender of your old beliefs which no longer serve you and keep you in limitation and ignorance. If you do this inner work of transformation, your ego will eventually unite with the Mind of God through the infusion action of Illumination. In the process of ascension, all aspects of you, including your human and ego mind, will unite completely with the Mind of God and all attributes of your divinity. Consider it an ongoing process for eternity, as there will always be another level, and another one, to open to and learn from. The process you need to surrender to will open your mind, your heart and all aspects of your divinity, but will not happen overnight. This is the journey you have created and planned for yourself before your incarnation in order to attain the goals you have set for your evolutionary pathway.

Gradually, you will integrate into your consciousness the knowledge, the understanding and the wisdom you need. As you do this, the veils will lift and you will unite your mind with the fullness of the Mind of God. If you don't wish to do your homework and you choose to stay in your present state, maintaining your erroneous concepts and belief systems, no one will force you to change. Be also aware that you will have to live with the consequences of being held back in your evolution while others you know and love will be lifted up into the next level.

Your own evolution is your primary goal for this incarnation and it requires your willingness and your effort to engage in it fully. It will not happen automatically. This really is a desire of the soul, and it should become the most profound desire and focus of your incarnation. This does not mean you cannot enjoy your third dimensional life. In fact, it is required that you love and enjoy your life to the fullest; it all needs to be integrated as one. Your transformation at this time of Earth's transition requires your full commitment and participation. This is the most important assignment and mission you can accomplish for yourself. Now it is time for you to set your priorities and become the masters you wish to be.

Group - How can we consciously evolve our human mind to unite with the Divine Mind?

Adama - Every day, invoke the energies of Illumination to unite with your human brain. Strive to expand your consciousness any way you can, such as reading material that inspires you, meditating, communing with nature, etc. You do not want to just feed the mind information, but you want to nourish your heart and soul with all that is noble, beautiful and enlightening. Go into your heart and begin to unite your energies with the Divine within you. In the process of ascension, your transformed mind will unite with the Sacred Heart; the heart will ascend first and you will experience divine union. All your chakras will become unified, and you will no longer feel separated from the rest of "you" and the universe. These will remain as different foci, but united at the same time. Many more chakras will be added to you and activated. You see how powerful that is. This is why an ascended master is an enlightened being. Do not wait for anyone's permission or nudging to start this process. Begin now if you want this Illumination to take place within you.

Group - If I were to call on the Illumination Ray during my sleep, what initiations would I be going through? Where would I be taken?

Adama - We suggest that you call the Illumination Ray during your waking time. In your sleep you know all of this. It is in the consciousness of your waking time that you need to integrate the wisdom you learn during your sleep time. Who you are on the other side of the veil, as the conscious self, is well informed and knows all.

Aurelia - I know that it is not necessary at this time that I consciously remember where I have been, what I have done and what I have learned during my sleep time. I feel it is more important that the knowledge I gained during night-time be integrated into my daily life.

Adama - Exactly. You are not meant yet to remember all your nightly adventures, because they are so wondrous. If you did remember now, it would create difficulty in remaining committed to completing your third dimensional experience. Such remembrance would set you back in your pathway. Once you set your intention with your guides and masters to do and learn certain things during your sleep time, they take you to all kinds of wondrous places that assist you to meet your goals, but you do not remember. For example, if you want to go to the Illumination Temple, they take you there. There is more than one on the planet, and you can visit them all if you wish. Actually, you have already done so more than once. But it is good for you to be aware that you can also go there consciously in your waking state. We have an Illumination Temple in our city. We have created a bridge of light between the temple in Telos and the one in South America. In our realm, they are not energetically separate; we all work together as one.

Group - Do we work on more than one Ray during a lifetime?

Adama - Not exactly.... In one incarnation most of you work on at least two Rays, a primary Ray and a secondary Ray in which you want to gain more attainment. Eventually you have to integrate and balance all of the Rays. In one lifetime you could be working on the Second or Third Ray, but you have had incarnations working on all the other Rays as well. The Ray that you are working on in this life is not necessarily indicative of your original monadic Ray. If you could read your akashic records, your monadic Ray, in which you were originally created, would be indicated by a tendency for more lifetimes to occur in that Ray. When you ascend, after mastering and balancing all the Rays, you usually return in service to your original monadic Ray.

Aurelia - How does the Illumination Ray balance our mental, emotional, physical and soul bodies?

Adama - The Illumination Ray alone does not balance all of your bodies. Its main purpose is to assist in the attainment of true wisdom, knowledge, illumination and the integration of the Divine Mind. Each Ray emphasizes a different action, but they all complement each other equally. Your world right now is flooded with misinformation. This is why right information is so needed and the development of discernment so important; both being Second Ray attributes.

Group - Adama, would Gandhi, Martin Luther King and John F. Kennedy be considered Second Ray beings?

Adama - John F. Kennedy was a First Ray being, the Ray of Leadership and of the Will of God. Gandhi was a Third Ray being of Love and Compassion. Martin Luther King was also a First Ray being. Leadership is mostly a First Ray activity, although not exclusively. Not only beings on the First Ray take roles of leadership in your world. Beings on all the Rays also bring their gifts in leadership roles from time to time in order for all of the Rays to be demonstrated. In order to ascend, you must gain mastery on all the Rays "equally."

Group - Can you explain the misuses of the Second Ray?

Adama - Some of the misuses of the Second Ray are using knowledge in the wrong way or entertaining conscious ignorance, such as not wanting to see things as they are. Entertaining illusions about life and self is also a misuse of the Second Ray.

We are going to talk for a moment about the heart. The human mind and the brain are third dimensional tools originally designed to be in service of the heart at all times. Your heart is connected to the divine Mind of God, and until you have reached a state of union with Self, your mental or ego mind needs to be consciously at the service of the heart. Eventually, it becomes a natural state of beingness. When you are working or acting through your human mind instead of your heart, and not in touch with the higher purposes of Life, that state of consciousness creates a misuse of the Second Ray, through spiritual ignorance, corruption control and manipulation of the ego mind. Some people have great human intelligence but have no spiritual wisdom. They often use that great intelligence in the service of the altered ego instead of seeking their Oneness with All That Is. The leaders of your governments, for example, know better than the actions they take and the way they choose to govern. You have access to much information about the corruption and secrecy taking place within your governments. These behaviors are dramatic misuses of the Second Ray and of leadership. Do you understand?

Aurelia - Yes. It sounds as if it could become quite devastating.

Adama - Well, it is the way it is. You can only change your own perspective on things and embrace the energies of love, peace and harmony for yourself first. Then when you own enough of these energies, you can radiate them to all others around you simply by being who you are. When everyone in the population starts accessing the Mind of God through the Heart, your governments will also begin to change and mirror the new consciousness of the collective. As you change, as the collective evolves its consciousness, so will your governments. This way, you begin to see that it is never about "them," but about all of you together. Your governments always reflect the consciousness of the people they govern. As you evolve, you will have the wisdom to elect more enlightened beings as your leaders. They are your mirrors.

Aurelia - What are the side effects of the misuse of the crown chakra and how would it show up in the physical body?

Adama - You know, the crown chakra is the instrument and the seat of the Mind of God in the physical body, designed to reflect knowingness, wisdom and illumination. Those who are consciously misleading people, controlling and manipulating, using their human knowledge for their own benefit only, eventually receive the harvest of their creation. They experience the return of their creation as karma. Some of the ways it may return can be as mental illnesses, such as Alzheimer's, Parkinson's, loss of memory or mental dysfunction or disease. As you get older, you are meant to get wiser and embrace more and more of the Mind of God. The opposite is quite prevalent in your society as people get older. Many people in nursing homes or mental institutions have reached such a state of mental deterioration, they are no longer able to relate to their own name or recognize their loved ones. On the human level, you can never judge anything because your judgments represent a very limited understanding.

Let us now do a meditation and go together to the Illumination Temple on the etheric plane.

Meditation to the Illumination Temple

Adama - First of all, we have an Illumination Temple in Telos, which is a smaller replica of the main Temple of Illumination for the planet at Lake Titicaca in South America. The majestic and awesome South American temple is maintained under the dedication and leadership of the God and Goddess Meru, very highly evolved beings who are custodians for the energies of that Ray for this planet. At this time, we are going to take you to the one in Telos which holds the same energy frequency. Our temple is vast with many facets, sections and chambers.

I ask you to focus in your heart, and set your intention to come along on a journey with us to the Temple of Illumination in our underground city. Ask your guides and your Higher Self to assist your consciousness to join us there. We have a huge merkaba that will comfortably transport all of you, and we invite you to step in for the ride.

Now perceive yourself arriving in Telos at the gateway of this temple. From a distance you are seeing an eight-sided golden yellow structure that radiates like a sun. It emanates its Illumination energy rays for several hundred miles into the atmosphere of the planet, and is also connected to the crystalline grid that distributes this energy everywhere on the globe very quickly.

See yourself walking up the 24 steps to this gateway of Light. As you set your feet on the last step, you are greeted by our people in Telos who are the gateway keepers. They invite you to step into a specific area of the foyer to be immersed in a shower of the Golden Light Ray that will clear and prepare your energy fields to be received in the temple.

At this point, each one of you is assigned a Lemurian guide who will escort and mentor you for your experience, as you now walk through the gateway. Then you are greeted on the other side by a most splendid team of Second Ray masters, the Planetary Christ, Lord Maitreya, Lord Buddha, and the Lords Sananda, Lanto, Confucius, Djwhal Khul and Kuthumi, extending to you all the love of their hearts.

They bid you their most heartfelt welcome into a beautiful entryway, like a huge portal, where everything you see radiates like a sun. There are no words in your language to describe what you see and experience, but this is not important. Use your imagination to create your experience more clearly. Imagination is a faculty of the Divine Mind, where all past and present experiences store their imprints, so that you can retrieve them later on in your conscious state. Allow your heart and consciousness to be bathed and imprinted with all that you see and perceive with the eyes of the soul. See how everything here reflects the golden sun of the love of the Creator for that Ray.

Notice and breathe in all the energies of the numerous fountains of golden liquid light that spring out from the center and along the walls of the great "Hall of Illumination." See the flowers of all colors, shimmering with tones of golden mist and exuding their heavenly scent everywhere. Imagine a wide variety of golden yellow flowers of different shades and sizes, growing together in a most stunning, harmonious and spectacular decor, creating a symphony of love, illumination and wisdom everywhere you look. Pay attention to the details of the floors, walls, and ceilings and all the beauty around you.

As you walk towards the front of a huge temple room, there is a large vessel where the Unfed Flame of Illumination is burning brilliantly. Also notice the masters of wisdom who stand around the great Illumination Flame in the center of the "Hall of Illumination." See how, by their constant outpouring of love, they create and nurture an ever spiraling expansion of that unfed Flame of Light. Without the nurturing of the Flames of God by those dedicated to this service, these various Flames would not exist and would be extinguished. The only source of fuel for these Flames comes from the fires of love and dedication that spring forth from the hearts of those who tend them. They keep these Flames alive and bright for the advancement of humanity and the benefit of the planet.

Keep breathing in deeply, beloved ones. This is a very special gift offered to you at this time. The doors of this temple are not always opened to unascended beings. You are here today by special dispensation and I encourage you to offer your deepest gratitude to Lord Maitreya and the other masters who have volunteered to hold the energies for you here, so that you may be allowed entrance. For those reading this material, if your desire is pure and sincere, the same dispensation will be accorded to you.

Continue to pay attention to the guide that has been assigned to you. Much wisdom and understanding can be shared through this interaction. Now you are invited to sit in a golden crystal chair in front of the master golden Flame. Feel the energy, feel the brilliant golden Flame penetrating every cell and particle of your ethereal body. We ask you to breathe in this energy as much as possible as you focus on this wonderful bright Flame of Illumination. Let it permeate all aspects of your being. This Flame stands about 60 feet tall, nourished around the clock by the love of our people, and that of the ascended masters and angelic beings.

As you focus on that Flame through the breath, connect in your heart with the Mind of God and the masters of Wisdom who nurture this Flame. Connect your heart with their hearts and ask them to imprint their love and dedication into your DNA and all your chakras. Ask for this light to infuse your mind with fifth dimensional wisdom.

Bring in your altered ego to this experience, as it is also divine and an integral part of you. It is not a part that you would get rid of, but the part of you that needs to be transformed back to its original purpose, and be reunited with the divine in the ascension process. This aspect of yourself needs to be understood and nurtured by your own self-love. Speak words of truth to your human mind and your altered ego and lovingly saturate these aspects of you with the Illumination Flame.

Speak to these parts of you with great love and compassion, as you would to a young adult or a child. Tell the human ego that it is also divine and loved, and ask it to surrender to the great wisdom of the Flame of Illumination to receive its love and comfort. Do this so that you can live your life with a greater integration of wisdom and inner knowingness.

When you go back to your body in daily life and are faced with making difficult decisions, bring into your sight this beautiful golden Flame of Illumination and Wisdom. Ask to be shown whatever you need to know in the now moment or for the choices you have to make. This is how you will come out of spiritual slumber, and this is also how you will learn discernment.

As your thoughts become one with God's thoughts, the Flames will assist you in their own unique ways to restore your spirit of limitlessness so that you can, once again, walk the Earth as wise masters and sages.

Ask for this energy and this knowledge to be integrated into your conscious mind. You may not remember all the details, but the knowledge will be imprinted in your soul; that is most important. You have carried in your soul so many erroneous belief systems which maintain you in pain and limitation. Ask that these be presented to the forefront of your awareness, then understood, cleansed and healed by the Illumination Flame. This process unfolds gradually, requiring your intention and your full participation. It is through the completion of this process that your ascension will become your reality and when you will take your place among the immortals.

Keep merging in ever greater measure with the Mind of God, which represents the intelligence of the heart. When you feel complete, stand up and walk around with your guide and ask questions for which you seek answers.

Carry on, resting your soul and your heart in that beautiful energy, which represents the sun of your divinity. It is through the Mind of God, through the Illumination Flame, that all knowledge will be accessed and delivered to your conscious mind when you align with it fully. The more you do this consciously through the heart, the greater and wiser beings you will all become, and the sooner we will be able to meet face to face. *(Pause)*

Now come back to consciousness and into your physical body. Intend to bring back with you as much as you can of your journey into the Temple of Illumination. Know that you now have permission to return there any time you wish as long as you remain in alignment with the love energies of the Second Ray.

There are a great number of masters of wisdom in the ascended state serving in the Temple of Illumination. They are also connected with the ashram of the Second Ray, where many souls come at night for classes and private tutoring, taking place in the Temple of Illumination. There are no fees for the classes, except for your willingness to love and to evolve your consciousness.

When you are ready, open your eyes. Be happy, grateful and harmonious with yourself and others. I thank you, dearest ones, for coming with us today. We send you our love, our wisdom, our support and our discernment. And so be it.

Aurelia - Thank you Adama, you are so very precious! And I thank you on behalf of the other participants today.

Adama - I am your mirror, my dearest ones. You are all so very precious as well.

Invocation to the Golden Flame of Illumination

Glorious Golden Flame of Illumination from the Heart of God in the Great Central Sun, I invoke the presence of beloved God and Goddess Meru into my heart, mind and soul. I ask you to flood my being with the precious oils of Illumination, poured over me in limitless radiance to transform all that is less than the divine perfection in my consciousness.

> O Flame of Light, so bright and radiant,
> O Flame of God, so wondrous to behold,
> Ceaseless fountains of wisdom flowing,
> Bring me back home to the heart of the sun!
>
> Come now with the fullness of thy power,
> Take my hand and open my eyes,
> Flooding my life with thy wonders,
> Blaze Illumination Flame through me!
>
> O Flame of Love, so wondrous to behold,
> Expand thy golden light through me today.
> Bless, heal, illumine and seal me,
> And all mankind, now and forever,
> In the Light of God that never fails.

Therefore, I choose to walk with God through the fires of Love from my heart. I am that God in manifestation and I acknowledge the mighty River of Radiant Golden Light of Illumination flowing through me.

I am this River of Light and I am this River of Golden Peace, now and forever.

I now intend that my entire consciousness, being and world be swallowed up in Light and bathed in the arms of Love. This world that I live in is full of Light, full of Love, and the Victory is assured. My own victory is assured because I am a divine love-illumination ray sending forth balms of divine healing to every part of myself and to every man, woman and child on this planet.

Chapter Fourteen

The Flame of Cosmic Love, A Third Ray Activity

With a Meditation to the Temple of Love

Adama with the Planetary Maha Chohan,

Paul the Venetian

Adama - Greetings, Aurelia, this is Adama. It is my understanding that you and your friends want to discuss the all-encompassing Flame of Love.

Aurelia - Yes Adama, it is my desire as well as those who are with me. There are already so many things that have been said and written about Love, and yet, it is not fully understood, even by the initiates. We, as humans on the surface, no matter how we strive to apply the consciousness of love, still often fall into duality and judgment. Please talk to us about Love once more, so that our hearts can be filled with the delicious nectar of that vibration.

Adama - My beloved sisters and family, I love you all so very much. All of us in Telos are so grateful for those like you who wish to understand the mysteries of Love at a much deeper level. Do not get discouraged; your full understanding is evolving. As you continue to strive to embody this wondrous energy, it continues to amplify within you. One day, in the not too distant future, it will be our great pleasure to invite you back among us, to the land of Love and Light. Thank you so much for giving me this opportunity to talk about Love. Though I am a Blue Ray Master, discussing the subject of Love always remains one of my favorites.

First of all, let me give you some background. The Flame of Love is one of the Seven Flames of God acting on this planet for humanity. The color of Love extends in great varieties of frequencies, tones and colors, ranging from a very light pink to the deepest golden ruby, in thousands of love-ray combinations. Love is the glue and the vibration that keeps all of God's creation functioning together in perfect order, harmony and majestic beauty. It is the master Paul the Venetian who now holds the office of the Chohan of the Third Ray of Love, having himself become the embodiment of the pure Flame of God's Love on the planet.

The Third Ray is connected to the heart chakra, magnifying the Love of the divine and human Self. Its divine qualities are, among many others, omnipresence, compassion, mercy, charity and the desire to be God in action through the love of the Holy Spirit.

Because of his great mastery of the eternal Flame of Cosmic Love, this master also holds the office of the Maha Chohan for the planet. In this position in the hierarchy, he is responsible at this time to embody the energy of what is known to you as the Office of the Holy Spirit. This is a very complex and wondrous office which could fill many chapters of a book. I want to announce that this great master has just entered the hall of our gathering and is gracing all of us with his presence. Welcome him in your heart. He is now blessing you with his radiance of pure love.

There are several retreats or temples of the Love Flame on the planet. We have a great temple of Love here in Telos, and there are temples of Love in all the subterranean and etheric cities of Light, not only on this planet, but throughout this and other universes. Paul the Venetian, a Frenchman in his last incarnation, is the guardian of an etheric retreat of the Third Ray below the Chateau of Liberty in Southern France. He has another retreat beneath the Temple of the Sun in New York City. There is a spiritual retreat of the Elohim of Love, Heros and Amora, twin flames of Love, around Lake Winnipeg, Manitoba, in Canada, and another awesome temple created and guarded by the Third Ray Archangels, twin flames of Love, Chamuel and Charity, in St. Louis, Missouri, USA.

Let me now speak of Love for a moment, as the only true and permanent force in all creation, and then I will invite Paul the Venetian to address you.

Love is not a word. It is an essence, a power and a vibration. It is Life! Love is the supreme element and vibration in all existence, an eternal dynamic living force. It is the golden chariot that transcends time and eliminates space. Love is the primal substance of Light out of which all things are created. It is the unifying power which holds all things together. Love simply contains everything. Enough intensity of love can heal and transform anything. Just as there is no real dividing barrier between your human self and your Grand Cosmic Self, there is no real dividing barrier between your human love and your Christ Love. There is only a difference in intensity and vibration. It is human love embodied and amplified a few million times.

There are those in incarnation who perceive love as a weakness. Love is certainly not a weakness, but the greatest strength. Love is the most important God-attribute that you can cultivate and develop. Its power can endure all things, rejoice in all things and glorify all things. Love is a constant force from which you can draw life's energies and harmony. Its healing tenderness penetrates all things and enfolds every heart. When one develops this great God-given faculty of Love, he will have the power to create and bring forth whatsoever his purified spiritual vision of love beholds.

For those who have perfected the fires of love, fear can no longer exist. Your higher Self has the ability to instantly transform huge quantities of human negativity into pure Love and Light. When the acquisition of this great gift of Love becomes the one main goal and desire in your life, when it has become a burning obsession that can no longer be denied, then it will be fulfilled. Such a one becomes the recipient of a Love so great that walls of glory are created around that individual, and nothing less than pure love can ever touch him/her again.

To those who attain this divine gift of Love, the realms of Light open wide and all powers are again bestowed upon them. Beauty, youthfulness and vitality in all their divine perfection, power and abundance in unlimited majesty, the all-knowingness of the Mind of God and all spiritual attributes restored in full measure are the gifts of perfected Love.

Pray to God and your divine Presence with all the energy of your heart to open yourself to this divine Christ-like love. Let this love begin to sing as a song of adoration and gratitude in your heart. Let your heart be lifted up continually by your heart songs of everlasting joy and gratitude, and this great love will become yours. Wherever you are, all powers and treasures of the higher realms will be bestowed upon you in heaven and on Earth, forever unto eternity.

These treasures of heaven are the divine gifts and qualities a man develops as he releases the hidden, God-given potentials within Self and within the Sacred Heart, the seat of your divinity. These gifts and powers that God holds forth for all of you are His plan for your full restoration as divine beings, as He waits patiently for you to fully accept them.

Within each one of you is held a cosmic bank account into which your merits are deposited or withdrawn. In the next world, mankind is not judged by his possessions, his human learning or his earthly position or honors. A man is judged by what he IS, by the level of his spiritual attainment. What he has become as a divine being is the only measure of evaluating the sum total of all he has thought, felt and done. This great Christ Light garment of pure Love, apparel of effulgent power and beauty, is brought forth from within as one begins to gather one's treasures in heaven. The glorified white raiment of Light that will be bestowed upon you is the outflowing interest that accrues from one's deposits of love, compassion, mercy, tenderness, gratitude and praise.

As you apply yourself to embody that Christ-like Love, rejoice in these great, dynamic treasures of fulfillment as heaven yields its wealth and its unlimited interest in your cosmic bank account, a hundred-fold multiplied! Yea, and so much more!

To give you some idea, most of the souls of humanity at the present time still have the Flame of Love burning in their heart at a level of $1/16^{th}$ to $1/8^{th}$ of an inch. Many of you who have been diligent and determined have reached a greater level, but you still have a ways to go. When the fires of Love within your heart burn a Flame that is nine feet tall, you will know that you have attained what it takes to finally be carried "home" on "Wings of Light" and be admitted among the immortals.

Aurelia - Wow, this sounds wonderful, Adama! I want to attain this. Thanks for reminding us again. I have known about this wondrous Love, but I have not yet fully understood it. What is keeping us from exploding into the fullness of our divinity, from this burning desire to realize perfected love?

Adama - There are several factors, and I am going to mention a few. You can figure out the rest. Not all apply to you personally, but in general, several of these factors apply to most people in various degrees. First, lack of vigilance and motivation, with too little faith in such promises. A lack of consistency in your resolution to invest enough time and energy in your spiritual development keeps you in a state of spiritual lethargy and in a spiritual negative balance. Your desires for love and ascension are still in a lukewarm stage.

Until it becomes a burning desire in your heart and soul, so great that you can no longer live without it, you cannot generate enough love, power and energy to attain this level of evolution.

I will say that most of you are suffering from a kind of spiritual laziness. You are all too busy "doing" rather than "becoming." For many of you who have laid out your spiritual goals, you are always looking for the latest excuse to procrastinate on your commitment to them. And this is without mentioning how many of you have not yet taken the time to seriously sit with "yourself" to write down your spiritual goals for your present incarnation. Have you seriously contemplated how you are going to reach those goals? How many of you possess a full understanding of why you have chosen to incarnate here at this time?

We suggest that you start now by slashing all your "to do lists" in half and investing in developing and integrating the love of your divinity. This takes time, love of self, effort and commitment on an ongoing basis; it simply does not happen on its own. You have left your evolution "to chance" too many lifetimes, and you are still here in pain and want. In truth, there is nothing more important for all of you at this time than this. Remember, all of what you do today and tomorrow and what you did yesterday has a very short-term impact on your lives. But what you "become" as a divine being incarnated in human experience remains with you for eternity. Which is more important?

You will say to me, "But Adama, we have to make a livelihood and take care of all our third dimensional obligations."

And I say to you, "Yes you do, and it is important for you to take care of your daily life with an impeccable spiritual perspective. It is in the context of daily life that you build your character and develop your God-given qualities."

If you prioritize your goals correctly and learn to manage your time appropriately, you will let go of your activities, social and otherwise, that from our perspective, are a pure waste of time and energy. All of you would be able to find at least one hour a day or more to invest in your spiritual life to commune with your divine Self and forging your mastery. If ascension is your intention and desire, it is imperative that you start managing your time more effectively. It is part of the curriculum of becoming a master of wisdom. Be creative! How do you expect to unite in love and divinity with an aspect of your Godhood, if you have no real interest in investing the time to get acquainted with it?

You can start speaking less and pondering more the wonders and splendor of the God-within. Meditate or contemplate your inner divinity while taking your nature walks. Cut most of your television and chitchat time, as these do not serve your spiritual evolution. Most of you can spend less time in stores. Nearly all of you have become addicted to shopping. Many of you spend too much time in the stores and shopping centers buying more things than you really need, which only adds to the clutter of your homes. This will save much money that you can use for more important endeavors. In the light realm, we are all so amazed and puzzled to observe how addicted to shopping this whole generation has become, constantly searching for new gadgets to buy. You get the picture, don't you? There are more human habits I could mention that keep you glued to the third dimension, but I leave it up to you to discover these.

Take time to review your life and know why you are here and where you are going. Take time to create a spiritual plan for yourself, and I promise you will never regret it.

There are three kinds of people in your world: those who make things happen, those who watch what happens and those who have no idea what happened. If you want to ride on the ascension wagon in this cycle, you must join those who make things happen. This means that you must actively pursue all that is required for your lifestream to be admitted into the great Halls of Ascension in this exceptional window of opportunity. Otherwise, it will simply not happen for you in this cycle, nor will it happen by association, but by your constant efforts and determination to create it.

You must stick with the process of purification and transmutation daily until your ascension becomes your reality. No matter what you have to go through at times to balance your debts towards life, if the fires of your hearts burn intensely enough, this love stands ready to see you through all potential tribulations with ease and grace.

Aurelia - You are very clear and concise in your explanations.

Adama - I am, because many of you are running out of time. You have been procrastinating far too long. You have less than five years to embrace the journey in order to attend the great planetary ascension party planned for the year 2012. Most of you underestimate the seriousness and the level of commitment required to make a physical ascension on a conscious level. Of course, there will always be another opportunity at a later time, and 2012 is not the end, but a beginning of an Ascension cycle for the planet. Those who are procrastinating now may not meet the requirements on time, and will certainly experience much regret.

Now I invite Paul the Venetian, who holds the office of the Maha Chohan *(representative of the Holy Spirit)* for the planet to speak to you.

Paul the Venetian - Beloved children of my heart! I greet you in the Flame of Love. May the blessings of the grace of the

Holy Spirit ever find me welcome within your heart, your feelings, and your very soul! Gentle as a pure white dove, which symbolizes His consciousness, the grace and humility of the Holy Spirit drawn out of the sweet delicate rhythm of its reverent song of being, are often overlooked by the Western mind. When a man comes to a place of "listening grace," when the restless energies of his many selves are stilled, then do the beauty, the grace, the benedictions and the presence of the Holy Spirit flow. As the wings of the dove carry her high, her freedom is manifest in "being," not so much in affirming or doing.

When one lives and serves according to the guidance of the Divine Self, there is happiness and fulfillment in that service. When one is developing new momentum, there are growing pains, and both are essential to mature consciousness. When the lifestream of the disciple is earnest and sincere, he makes the effort to always be in the perfect place where the wisdom of the I AM Presence requires him to be. Life will then always cooperate and guide that lifestream where the greatest service and advancement can be rendered.

Our words are crystal cups that carry love and peace into the outer consciousness of those of mankind who have a remembrance of spiritual friendship and sweet association with us at inner levels. Through the magnetic power of the Threefold Flame within the Heart, the attention of the masters of the higher realms can be drawn to you for greater assistance.

One of the main sources of unhappiness, frustration and distress experienced by mankind is the capacity and willingness to disobey the divine directions of their own individualized I AM Presence and the guidance of the Ascended Hosts of Light. There is always a choice between joyous, willing, illumined obedience to the directions of that Presence and the willful and ignorant misuse of the free will to create imperfection. It becomes a personal choice and matter between each man and his God.

However, until each member of the human race comes to a personal desire to do the Will of God and live by the laws of Love, he will not experience permanent happiness or the joy of victorious accomplishment, which brings peace, abundance, limitless love and a spiritual expansion not yet known to your outer mind.

Man did not destroy the conscious connection with his own individualized I AM Presence in a moment, nor can he re-establish such a connection in a moment. It requires patience, persistence, determination, purity of motive, a well-developed sense of discrimination and constant vigilance at the door of the heart of the Presence.

The Presence of God is waiting, waiting for the opportunity to serve through you. The beautiful, loving, all-powerful Father of Life stands in a constant attitude of listening. Whenever He is called, He answers with an onrush of His mighty Presence through the instruments created and prepared by His love.

Beloved children of the Father/Mother of Life, could your eyes but see the imminence of the Holy Presence when your innocent forms rise from their beds and place their feet upon the pathway of the day, you would understand the rudeness of the outer self in keeping the Presence waiting. In the press of unimportant things, sometimes a day, a week or a lifetime passes, and the Presence of God is still waiting for the opportunity to fill your cup with grace, peace, abundance, healing and love.

And so, my beloved children, proceeding through the veil of human experience, remember, when your feet step upon the ground each morning that the Presence of God is waiting to fill your day with the fullness of your divinity, if you choose to invite it! Remember today, as you read these lines, the Presence of God is waiting to bless each one of you with the fullness of the Love and Peace beyond all understanding.

Invoke that Presence each day and each hour of the day to be filled with the Love, Peace and Harmony that will grace your lives with the experience of ease and perfection.

Codes of Conduct for a Disciple of the Holy Spirit

The Maha Chohan

1. Become conscious always of your aspiration to embody the full expression of Godhood, and devote all of your being and service to that end.

2. Learn the lessons of harmlessness—neither by word, nor thought, nor feeling will you ever inflict evil or harm upon any part of life. Know that action and physical violence will keep you in the realm of pain, suffering and mortality.

3. Stir not a brother's sea of emotion thoughtlessly or deliberately. Know that the storm in which you would place his spirit will sooner or later flow upon the banks of your own lifestream. Rather bring always tranquility, love, harmony and peace to all life.

4. Disassociate yourself from the personal and planetary delusion. Never allow yourself to love your little self more than the harmony of the universe. If you are right, there is no need to acclaim it. If you are wrong, pray for forgiveness.

5. Walk gently upon the Earth and through the universe, knowing that the body is a sacred temple, in which dwells the Holy Spirit, bringing peace and illumination to life everywhere. Keep your temple always in a respectful and purified manner, as befitting the habitation of the Spirit of Love and Truth. Respect and honor with gentle dignity all other temples, knowing that often within a crude exterior burns a great light.

6. In the presence of Nature, absorb the beauties and gifts of Her kingdoms in gentle gratitude. Do not desecrate Her by vile thoughts, sounds or emotions, or by physical acts that despoil Her virgin beauty. Honor the Earth, "the Mother" that is hosting your evolutionary pathway.

7. Do not form nor offer opinions unless invited to do so, and then, only after prayer and silent invocation for guidance. Speak when God chooses to say something through you. At other times it is best to speak little, or to remain peacefully silent.

8. Let your heart sing a song of gratitude and joy unto God. Be grateful always for all that you have received and that you have in the now moment. Tap in to the River of Life, River of Love and Abundance that lies within the Sacred Heart.

9. In speech and action be gentle, but with the dignity that always accompanies the Presence of the living God that lives within the temple of your being. Constantly place all the faculties of your being and all the inner unfoldment of your nature at the feet of the God-power, endeavoring to manifest the perfection of compassion when meeting those in distress.

10. Let your word be spoken in gentleness, humility, and loving service. Do not allow the impression of humility to be mistaken for lethargy, for the servant of the Lord, like the sun in the heavens, is eternally vigilant and constantly outpouring the gifts of Love to those who open their hearts to receive them.

Meditation

Journey to the Crystal-Rose Flame Temple of Love

ᴊ𝘈dama

This is one of the etheric temples of the Love Ray, guarded and maintained by the Love Flame of the archangels of the Third Ray, Chamuel and Charity. This temple is situated over the city of St. Louis, Missouri. An arc of divine love forms a bridge between this retreat and that of the Elohim of the Third Ray, Heros and Amora, in the etheric realm near Lake Winnipeg in Canada.

The emanation of the Love Ray from this specific temple is a flow of creativity. The Flame of Love from this retreat promotes the generosity of the heart, givingness, forgivingness and mercy. The enormous energy of Love simply flushes out all else and assists the people who visit this temple to retain more of the qualities of Love for themselves and for the world. The altar and flame of the retreat are dedicated to the flow of life from the heart of the Creator, to the heart of Christ, and then to the heart of man.

Now, my beloveds, come with me, accompanied by the energy of the Holy Spirit through the love of the Master Paul the Venetian, to that specific Temple of Love.

Close your eyes and take a few deep breaths. Set your intention to come along with us in the etheric vehicle we are now presenting to you. You are traveling in your light body vehicle. You may or may not have a conscious remembrance of this, but the benefits are the same. Use the gift of your imagination to create a vivid impression of what we describe, and the journey will remain imprinted in your soul and cellular memory. When needed, you will be able to access, not necessarily the recollection of all the details, but certainly the energies you will receive through this experience.

175

Also know that the more you apply yourself in taking these types of journeys, the more you are assisting the thinning of your own veil of illusion which blocks your memories and perception of the higher vibrations. Ask your Higher Self to facilitate this journey for you and with you, and open your heart to experience this on the inner planes at the highest possible level.

We are now traveling through space from your home in Mount Shasta to the magnificent Crystal-Rose Flame Temple of Love. Take in the fragrance of the crystal-rose petals of love all around you, even before you arrive. You are so very blessed, for such a small group to have the privilege of being accompanied personally by the planetary representative of the Holy Spirit Himself. Indeed, this is a rare occurrence. Let me share with all of you now present that it is your love and your staunch devotion to your pathway that is allowing Him to grant you this grace.

Breathe in, my beloveds. Relax and allow the experience fully. Deepen your breath to take in all you can, in order to bring back with you the greatest soul imprint that you can create. This will assist you and enhance your pathway in a more harmonious and direct way. *(Short pause)*

Now we are here in front of the large translucent crystal-rose, multi-layered dome. It is like nothing you have ever seen before in your outer world. There are no words in your language to describe the structure, so beautiful and elegant, fashioned by the creativity of the archangelic love of Chamuel and Charity.

Beam Rays of pure Love energy emanate from the central point of the dome to radiate the Love of the Creator hundreds of miles into the atmosphere in all directions. A most wondrous scene to behold, dear ones!

Allow yourself to walk on the velvety crystal-rose carpet

that is extended beneath your feet to the doorway of the temple. Because we are in the company of the Maha Chohan Himself, you will not be required to show your passport of entry to be admitted here. Because archangelic frequencies are so high and rarefied, no soul is permitted to come here unless they are able to maintain at least fourth dimensional frequencies of love and harmony at all times, and are accompanied by one of the Masters of Wisdom.

As you get close to the entranceway, several angels of the Love Ray, about 12 feet tall, bow to the great Light of the Maha Chohan. They also bow to my Light and to your own Light as well, inviting you to enter.

Each of you is escorted by one of these temple guardians. This temple is three times larger than the Vatican of the Catholic Church in Rome and contains many sections of various dimensional energies for the numerous activities of the temple.

You are taken to an area which will be comfortable for your own level of heart evolution. You are now crossing a long corridor filled with thousands of love-flame angels of all sizes. These angelic beings vary from the smallest cherubim to the largest seraphim. Actually, all 12 choirs of the angelic kingdom from all dimensions are represented here.

As you walk the corridor, a large number of fountains and cascades of pure Love energy spring forth from various places. The energies that emanate from these fountains and cascades sing their songs of Love and Gratitude perpetually to the heart of the Creator, to the Mother and to all kingdoms, including humanity, evolving on this planet in all dimensions. If you allow it, these melodies of Love can melt much of the dross that your heart has accumulated and carried for so very long. Listen and let your hearts merge with the energies of the love songs coming from the Waters of the Eternal Rivers of Love.

Pure white doves of Love, much larger than the ones you know on the surface, send you their healing radiance. Take your time to look, feel and observe the wonders of God's Love waiting to be bestowed upon those who love Life and obey the Eternal Laws of Love. No one is rushing you. Remember, you are here in a zone of timelessness. Also listen to the love songs of the wide varieties of Third Ray flowers, plants and fruit gracing this temple pathway. Allow yourself to receive healing from the sweetness of the fragrance and melodies. The doves also want to connect with your heart to comfort the rest of your journey back to the "Sun of your Presence." Walking this corridor that portrays the energies of pure magical Love is part of your experience here. If you have any questions, each of you has your own angelic guide waiting so willingly to answer them. *(Pause)*

See now an entrance on the right. Your guides are bidding you to follow them into the Hall of the Eternal Flame of Cosmic Love. This is another unfed Flame that is perpetually burning to glorify the Creator, the Father of All. By cosmic law, all planets receiving the love and energies of the Creator must return to Him a portion of it each day, produced by the fires of the hearts of those who inhabit those planets. On this planet, since surface humanity has neglected to do this for eons of time while journeying in warring and separation, we in Telos, with many beings from the Inner Earth and other subterranean cities, have done this on your behalf. We will continue to do so until the day that all of you attain enough spiritual maturity to return this level of grace and gratitude to the Creator yourself.

Those serving in the Crystal-Rose Temple, do this as their service to Life, also feed the Eternal Flame of Love through the love fires of their hearts. When we say unfed Flame, we mean that what nourishes and tends the fire of Love and keeps the Flame burning perpetually is the Love from the Hearts of those who serve in the temple. In fact, all the Love temples holding the same energy create a web of Love nourishing and supporting the civilizations and various kingdoms living here on this Earth.

This Flame, ever so gentle and powerful, stands a hundred feet or more in height and about nine feet in diameter. The source of its strength is the power of gentleness. It is blissful, joyous and playful. It contains all that the Creator can bestow on His Creation and the many children of His heart. It is limitless.

Take time now to breathe it in even more deeply. Connect deeply with the Flame and allow it to fill your heart to the brim, and relax in the arms of Love. How wondrous! *(Pause)*

When you feel that your heart has been filled to full capacity, walk quietly back to the crystal merkaba waiting for you outside to bring you back to your physical body. In deep gratitude, thank Paul the Venetian for the Grace he has accorded you today, and in the future for those who will be working with the written material. When you are ready, open your eyes and come back to your body.

With these words, we now conclude our meditation. I urge you to return there in consciousness whenever you feel you need to boost the fires of your heart. In Telos we love you so very much. Our love will accompany your steps unto the end of your journey.

Aurelia - On behalf of the small group here, I thank you Adama very profoundly for all that you do for us, and I also thank Paul the Venetian for the Love, the Grace and the Blessings He has bestowed upon us today.

Adama - You are welcome, my beloveds!

When a man comes to a
Place of "listening grace,"
When the restless energies
Of his many selves are stilled,
Then does the beauty, the grace,
The benedictions and the presence
Of the Holy Spirit flow.
As the wings of the dove carry her high,
Her freedom is manifest in "being,"
Not so much in affirming or doing.
- Maha Chohan, Paul the Venetian

Chapter Fifteen

The Ascension Flame of Purification and Transformation, A Fourth Ray Activity

With a Meditation to the Ascension Temple in Telos

Adama with Serapis Bey

Peace and love from the Heart of Lemuria, this is Adama with the Chohan of the Fourth Ray, our beloved Serapis Bey. I bring you the blessings of my Light and the victory that lies within it. We bid you our most heartfelt welcome.

Today, we wish to talk about the Ascension Flame, a most wondrous action of the sacred fire that can facilitate your pathway to your ascension. When you possess a more specific understanding of how to consciously use this glorious Flame of purification, you can accelerate the cleansing process of all your chakras, the activation of your DNA, and prepare the cells of your various bodies for a physical ascension. This is magnificent, my friends, to say the least.

In the land of Egypt, along the banks of the Nile River, there exists a focus of the Great White Brotherhood of Light, dedicated to preserving the Cosmic Flame of Ascension, which is "The Way Back Home" for every lifestream. Present with me at this time is Master Serapis Bey, the guardian director or Chohan of this magnificent Ascension Temple at Luxor. He has been holding this position in service to our planet since the destruction of Atlantis.

He is here today with his team of ascended masters who specialize in this service. They are known as "The Ascension Brotherhood." All these masters extend to you the elixir of their heart's love through the purifying fires of the Ascension Flame. Breathe this in, my beloveds; this is a gift to you. These dedicated beings have worked closely with our brother Serapis Bey for several centuries, planning the evolution of the human race for this time that has finally come. Their service to Life at this time is to engage their energies in preparation for lifting the planet and the consciousness of humanity into ascension.

The Ascension Temple at Luxor sustains the pulsation of the Ascension Flame into the atmosphere of Earth; our Ascension Temple in Telos sustains the Sacred Flame in the very same way. Visualize two temples, united in consciousness and energy, blessing and loving daily and hourly everything on Earth for the benefit of ascending humanity.

With each successive spring season, this Sacred Flame is freely and widely utilized by the beings of the nature kingdoms to renew and resurrect the beauty of Nature everywhere. Each soul on Earth desiring and applying to complete their cycle of incarnation by the process of Ascension is placed under the tutelage of the Ascension Brotherhood and the Office of the Christ.

A few hundred years ago, a great portion of the activities and records held in this great pyramid at Luxor for so long were either transferred or duplicated in Telos. This relocation was implemented because the spiritual hierarchy of the planet foresaw future potential problems in this area of the globe. All the records and energies of that sacred focus could not be compromised in the event of regional or global cataclysms on the horizon then. Now Telos has become a main focus of Ascension for the planet in total cooperation with the great masters of Luxor. We all work together in perfect harmony for the benefit of the collective. This is one of the fifth dimensional protocols.

The decision was made that a part of this important planetary focus would be safer underground, and best guarded in its original purity and sacredness, nurtured and honored by the large number of ascended beings in Telos.

Although it may seem that there are now two Ascension focuses on the planet, I say that for us it is only one. In the dimension where we function, time and space as most of you understand it do not exist. It is all one.

After the sinking of Atlantis and Lemuria, the surface populations have continued to war against each other to this day. For this, my beloveds, keep up your hope and courage. You know that it will not be tolerated much longer; this consciousness will come to an end and be healed.

In Telos, soon after the destruction of both continents, we volunteered for the task of keeping the Flame of Ascension on behalf of mankind, as part of our service to this planet, in order to insure its continuity. This is why we have been granted the opportunity for such a service. From the Love of our Hearts, we extend to you this day your own opportunity to embrace and expand this wondrous Flame within your hearts for your own Ascension. We say to you that the heart ascends first, and the rest follows.

Although everyone will eventually reach this state in their own unique way and timing, there are standards and frequencies of Light that can never be compromised by any of us in order to maintain our level of attainment. The same is also required for all those aspiring for Ascension. You must be willing to walk all the steps to your homecoming and be able to maintain the ascended state frequency as your permanent state of beingness.

Aurelia - Is a large percentage of humanity going to ascend by 2012?

*Adama - It is not yet known how many people will ascend with the planet by the year 2012. We perceive a potential of a few million out of 7 billion on the planet, but this number is subject to change at any time according to individual and collective choices. We often hear those calling themselves "lightworkers" saying that by the year 2012, all of humanity will ascend to the fifth dimension unconditionally, and that no one will be left behind. And we say back to you, "Not so." No one will be left behind ultimately, but everyone must do their own inner work to evolve their consciousness to that level and balance their debts to life before being invited into the great "Halls of Ascension."

Although there is greater assistance being offered to humanity than ever before in all of Earth's history, and the Ascension process is made easier than ever before, none of you will be lifted into Ascension until you meet all the requirements and reach the necessary frequency. It does not matter how long it takes for you to reach this consciousness in the cycles of time, one or more incarnations, the laws of the dimensions are always applied. For those in great resistance, it may take several more incarnations. The opportunity is offered to all, but not all will choose it.

It is required of those aspiring for Ascension that you heal and transform all your erroneous belief systems and embrace love, harmlessness, and the truth of your divinity. Realize that the year 2012 is not the end of the Ascension cycle on this planet, but simply a wondrous beginning. The full planetary process for the Earth, in the completion of Her full glory and destiny, is a 1,000-year plan, and perhaps even longer.

In 2012, it is the Earth, Herself, that is making her glorious Ascension in the Light, along with those who have met all the necessary requirements.

In the years following 2012, all souls in incarnation on Earth will continue their evolution and ascend only when they have met all the requirements. For some it may take 6 months, for others 2, 5 or 8 years, and for many, 20 to 50 years or longer.

You will need to fully engage yourself in the initiation process leading to Ascension, and to successfully meet all the prerequisites for this graduation. Each one's journey is unique, and though the initiatic process is similar for everyone, it unfolds differently for each soul, according to their own distinctive pathway.

It is true that everyone, without exception, is offered the opportunity for Ascension at this time, but be aware that many souls are making other choices. Those beloved souls who choose to continue to experience separation are not yet ready for this evolutionary step and will be given the opportunity to continue their evolution at their own pace somewhere else. The grace of Ascension will be offered to them again at some later time when they request it. Eventually, everyone will return to the frequency of the Love of the Heart of the Creator. In this way, no one will be left behind. As the beloved children of your Creator, you have been created out of the most magnificent Love vibration, and to this Love vibration you are also destined to eventually return.

Aurelia - Adama, can you give us a description of this Flame?

Adama - This Flame contains the frequency and color of all the other Flames. You see or experience it as a brilliant, luminous, dazzling white light that consumes on contact all that is less than the perfection of Love. Its power and brilliance is limitless. It sustains worlds in perfect harmony and beauty.

Those invoking and working with it must be prepared for change. When touched by this Flame, you are never the same again. Everyone can work with it, of course, but in its full intensity, it holds the capacity to completely transform the initiate who has reached the doorway of Ascension. When you are finally ready to take this leap in your evolution, you will be immersed in the frequency of that magnificent ascension energy. It will propel you into the final step, where the fires of that Love will consume all human limitations, your full consciousness will be restored, and your body will be fully immortalized. You will then be invited to join the "immortals" as an ascended master, stepping into that most glorious state of spiritual freedom and conscious reconnection with your Creator and with all that exists within His heart. This is how powerful, my friends, the Ascension Flame is.

Aurelia - How can we consciously reach this level of frequency and maintain it?

Adama - This information has been given to people of Earth for a very long time, again and again, and in this age through a wide variety of writings and channelings. It has been presented to you in so many packages and colors that you fail to recognize it. Unless a teaching and key of wisdom is thoroughly learned and integrated through the heart, it remains "just information" in the clutter of your mind that you soon forget. Ultimately, it does not advance the evolution of your consciousness. We know people who have read hundreds of spiritual books; they have a lot of mental knowledge, but since they have not integrated this knowledge to embody their divinity, their spiritual progress remains marginal.

In fact, you are bombarded with much information through the many books you read and the many seminars and conferences you attend. For many of you, it has remained to this day simply "information" that your mind is unable to process, let alone integrate. Only your heart can do the job, not your human mind.

Allow me to repeat what we have said before, and what others have also mentioned, hoping that if we repeat this often enough, it will eventually sink in for you to maintain the frequency from the efforts you invest in your evolution. We have often said that "Ascension" does not require the doing of so many things, but is about becoming, embracing and remembering to live your lives as the God/Goddess that you are. It means fully embracing the divinity that already exists within you through the expansion of your consciousness as Beings of Love and Compassion, and living from the wisdom of the heart. It is that simple, my beloveds. If you become this, you do not need anything else. All this already exists and lives within you. I remind you that there is nothing outside the Self.

Here are some of the main points or guidelines to be understood and considered about the initiatic path leading to your graduation from Earth's curriculum through the Ascension protocols.

- This process is one of complete purification and healing of all that hinders your transfiguration, resurrection and ascension into the arms of God/ Love; the restoration of your dignity and memories, so that you live, once again, as divine children of your heavenly Father/Creator, entering the world of "Oneness."

- Understand that each dimension represents a certain frequency. The fifth dimension becomes accessible to you when, and only when, you have attained that frequency in your consciousness and have the ability to maintain it at all times.

- Live from the heart, speaking and acting as a master would, at all times, as a way of "being." Always ask yourself the question, "What would a master do or say in this or that situation?" Then go within and find the answer. If it is not clear, take a piece of paper and pen, light a candle if you wish, and set your intention to find the answer inside of you. The master within is awake and alert at all times, forever waiting for your recognition.

- Let go of the third dimensional consciousness of separation, duality, polarity and drama in all its myriad forms. Stop believing in two powers, and giving your powers and precious energy away to the power of illusion of this third dimensional density. Allow yourself to set aside all that you have learned so far that has not given you the results you are yearning for. Be ready and willing to learn anew, and have the courage to step into the unknown reality of Love and Magic. Recognize that Love is the only true power there is, and start living your life from the inside out in that vibrational frequency.

- Let go of all judgment and expectation about yourself and others, and how life should be unfolding for you. Allow yourself to perceive and embrace all the wonders and majesty of "YOU" in the splendor of your divinity, and accept the great adventure of letting it unfold and transform in front of your eyes, in deep joy and gratitude.

- Embrace the banner of humility and the sweet surrender to one's holy vows. If you don't know what they are, they are written within your very cells and DNA, as well as in many chambers of your Sacred Heart. Be willing to take the time to go within and do some investigation.

- Establish a conscious union with your great I AM Presence and the fulfillment of your divine plan. The Ascension is the unification, the merging into divine union with your magnificent I AM Presence. In order to embody this glorious aspect of yourself, it is an obvious requirement that you make yourself familiar and intimate with that aspect of Self you want to merge with. How can you expect to ascend and unify with an aspect of Self you have not taken the time to know and understand?

The answers we receive amaze us when we ask people in channeling sessions what the ascension represents to them. We get answers such as ascension means changing dimension, being able to manifest everything, not having to be limited by money anymore, being able to teleport, and so on.... Although these are the gifts and results of ascension, they are not the primary purpose. The focus is YOU, your level of understanding your divinity and becoming it in your daily life.

- Embrace the consciousness of harmlessness by honoring the sanctity of all life forms sharing this planet with you, and the divine right of every person living here.

- Release old programming running your life and all negative emotions stored in your conscious, unconscious and subconscious memories, including the balancing of all debts to life. You have already had many teachings on these topics.

- When individuals feel they have incurred heavy debts towards life in the past, they often become obsessed with the idea of heavy karma. They create a certain lethargy in the feeling body blocking their ability to begin clearing their debt.

• When individuals believe their debt to be light and they enter into the spirit of releasing it steadily into the sacred fire, they create a great release of joy that flows through their being. The feeling of joy within your consciousness has a tendency to create malleability in the coil of energy that keeps the records of the debts. This relaxes the tensions within the energetic coils, and frees the individual to move on more quickly through all initiations with greater ease and grace.

• The attitudes that will assist anyone the most to move through the balancing of their shadow creation are twofold. The main one is to adopt as a way of life to do everything you do, at all times and in every moment, no matter what happens, as an act of love, for yourself, for your fellowmen, for the planet, for the other kingdoms sharing the planet with you and for creation itself. And secondly, the attitude of gratitude will assist you immensely.

• Nurture and expand a genuine desire for your ascension and immortality by embracing the willingness to walk the path unto the end! Unless you entertain in your consciousness a genuine desire for ascension and immortality, and unless you are willing to shed the old ways of living in the third dimension which have kept you and humanity in pain for so long, and unless you walk the path shown to you by the masters of wisdom who have gone before you, you will not become a true candidate for Ascension.

In seeking Ascension, the power of Love must become the fervent heat which causes the elements of mortal creation to melt, and which will propel the candidate for Ascension into the great cosmic pool of immortal Love and Light.

Serapis Bey - For those calling themselves seekers of truth who yearn for contacts with the Hierarchy of Light and the Great White Brotherhood, it is required that you come directly under the guidance and the tutelage of the great master teachers. The path of mastery, achievement, freedom, victory and ascension can only be achieved through the initiatic process. For all great masters who have ever ascended on this planet, or elsewhere, the Flame of Ascension has always been a most important key which unlocks the door of immortality for every soul.

I have guarded, I have guided and stood within the Ascension Flame for a very long time, in order that there might be a way and means by which humanity, when complete with the folly of the senses, could return to their Divine estate. Since the "fall of man," had there not been a guarding Brotherhood of the Ascension Flame, there would be no way back home for humanity. Have you ever pondered within the deepest recesses of your being how it would be if no way back home had been created by the dedication and love of the Masters who have ascended before you?

To this end, we have remained, many of us, prisoners of Love upon this temporary dark Star. The Lemurian Brotherhood of Light of Telos eventually joined us in our vigil of Ascension for the planet. Together, we have kept the Flame of Love and Light on behalf of mankind for thousands of years, until the day when you mature enough to partake in this planetary responsibility.

I am dedicated to see that you pass through the fires of purification. For those who have applied for the opportunity of attaining the ascended status, I will remain firm and vigilant until that glorious victory becomes your reality. We are heart-friends of many ages.

Quote from Lord Jesus/Sananda

"Knowing the supreme glory of that hour, I can but urge each dear child of God to prepare for that glorious moment! When the hour comes and the summons from the Father of Light reaches your heart, you will also know the full and true purpose for human incarnations. It is to prepare your consciousness to become a Sun of Light within yourself, free of the wheel of birth and death, and a master of energy and vibration."

Those interested in visiting the Ascension Temples at Luxor and Telos are requested to bring back with them in their consciousness that rising, buoyant, joyous energy which is the activity of Ascension. This Flame will enter into the elemental substance of the inner bodies, as well as the physical form, and act as the "leaven in the loaf," when earnestly invoked. As the pure white Flame passes through the substance of the aspirant's bodies—physical, mental, emotional and etheric—it quickens the vibratory action of the atom, each electron moving more rapidly around its own central pole. This causes the throwing off of the impure, discordant substances around the electron, and quickens the rhythm of all the vehicles. These vehicles then become more sensitive to the finer vibrations of the higher spheres. Their consciousness becomes more attuned to Truth, the gravity pull is lessened, and the various distorted and erroneous beliefs of the ego are lessened.

To ascend to the state of self-mastery, God wisdom, peace, harmony, perfect health, limitlessness, and ever-present supply, the candidate for the great gift of Ascension must learn to rely totally upon the Presence of God within the heart. The disciplines of the Ascension Brotherhood are designed to turn the consciousness from the outer world "inward," until, from within the heart center, the seat of your divinity, there is drawn forth and at will anything and everything which is required to manifest the fullness of your Divine Essence in physical manifestation. All must be purified and transformed through the ascending fires of that Royal Flame!

Meditation and Journey to the Ascension Temple in Telos

Adama and Serapis Bey

Along with our honorable guests here this evening, twelve members of the Ascension Brotherhood of Luxor, we now invite you to come with us on a journey to the Ascension Temple of Telos. If you desire this initiation, as would a master, set your intention in your heart with your Higher Self and guides to come along with us for this experience. Your souls are already rejoicing.

A dazzling white light merkaba from the fifth dimension is now approaching to take, in their etheric bodies, those who choose to come. Now step through intention into that vehicle of light and take your seat. We ask you to prepare yourself by centering within, and allow yourself to feel and perceive the buoyant and joyous energies of this Flame already enfolding you. We ask that through this journey, you breathe as deeply as you can, in order to take in and bring back to your outer awareness the energies of this Flame. This experience is an opportunity to ignite another level of the purification process for every cell, atom and electron of your main and subtle bodies.

Youp! Since we are not very far away, we are already there. Open yourself to this experience as consciously as you can, and enjoy! This temple is huge, a very tall scintillating white light pyramid with four sides. If you have been to the one in Egypt, you will see that it is not exactly the same, but similar in many ways. Of course, the fifth dimensional aspects of these two ascension pyramids are even more glorious, elegant and magnificent than the third dimensional counterpart visible in Egypt. The one in Telos does not have a third dimensional counterpart as the one at Luxor, its power and beauty are stunning.

Step off the merkaba and come with us to the "Hall of Transfiguration," where each one of you will be introduced to the Ascension Brotherhood guide who will assist and escort you during your experience here.

Feel the air, the energies, the power and the brilliance of this holy place. We encourage you to pay attention to your guide and ask any question you want clarity on. This is your experience, beloveds, and you create it in any way you wish. Our role is simply to accompany you with our love and wisdom.

At times, you are almost blinded by such brilliance, and this is good. You are now walking through a corridor of exquisite beauty, leading to the atomic accelerator chamber. Continue to fill your lungs and consciousness with this beauty and joy. As you walk along, there are many beings who serve in this temple or are visiting here, who notice you and greet you with their smiles and gestures of friendship. All of them, in their own way, welcome you and send you their blessings. The halls of this temple are usually open only for those whose candidature for ascension has been accepted.

The guardians of the atomic accelerator chamber bid you welcome and you are now entering this great hall with your guide. What you see is a very large room that contains several hundred small dazzling white crystalline pyramids circling the main focus of that Flame in the center of the room. You are almost overtaken by the wonder and magnificence of the immortal unfed Flame of Ascension burning bright in front of you, almost 200 feet tall and 100 feet in diameter at the base.

Its power almost overwhelms you and once you have a deep experience of this Flame in your energy fields, you will never be quite the same again, unless you consciously choose to return to your former level of resonance. In spite of its great rushing power, it does not emit any noise, except the melodious sounds of music created by this energy field. Also notice the sweet fragrance that facilitates the raising of your frequency emanating from the energies of the Ascension Flame.

With your guide, you now walk around the base of the Flame to fill yourself with all the spiritual gifts you can receive here today. Now your guide, who has already chosen one of the smaller pyramids for you, invites you to step in for your next experience. Each one of these small pyramids of light contains an atomic activator, on which you sit, that will assist you to raise your vibration to a comfortable level. These accelerators have been designed in such a way that they could raise you all the way to the Ascension frequency and immortality, but this is not the goal of the experience at this time. You are here to experience "a little push" to your next level. It is different for each one. The level of acceleration each one will receive is calibrated to their level of initiation and readiness on their pathway.

Do not worry. As much as some of you would love to experience the full Ascension at this time, you will not disappear; we guarantee that you will return to your physical bodies in good shape and charged with a new and purer vibration in your auric field. It will be up to you from then on to use this experience to the best of your ability as another step forward, or quickly forget what you have received, and maintain the status quo. It is all up to you—we are only your facilitators.

What is an atomic accelerator? For those of you not yet familiar with this concept which the Master Saint Germain has spoken about quite widely in his channelings of the last century, let us describe it briefly. He is one of the designers of this technology. The atomic accelerator does exactly what its name suggests. It is a crystalline seat or chair designed with a technology that creates the frequency of the Ascension Flame for those sitting upon it. Like many of your instruments, it possesses a control dial, and as you meditate on this Flame and pour the love of your heart into it, you are infused by your guide with its frequency at the exact level that best serves you in the now moment. Your guides already know the frequency that is best for you, and they are well trained in applying it.

This type of technology is not available yet in your dimension. It has the ability to transform into perfection every element vibrating at a frequency less than the pure Love essence of the Creator. One can literally and symbolically say that it has the ability to transform base metals into the purest gold. In other words, when the time comes for you to make your Ascension, it will transform your mortal body with all its imperfections and limitations into your perfect, immortal deathless solar body of light, in all its majesty and splendor.

As you continue to sit on the seat assigned to you, keep breathing in, while communing with your Divine Essence and with your Creator. Set your goals of Ascension for this life and open your heart to your God. *(Pause for integration)*

When you feel that you are finished, look into the eyes of your guide and receive the love that he/she chooses to impart to you through the eyes of his/her soul, as you express your gratitude. When you feel ready, stand up and direct your consciousness to exit with your guide from the chamber you are in, and retrace your steps to the merkaba that brought you here. We are now bringing you back to this room with your auric fields and hearts filled with a new love and a new light vibration. It is really up to you to maintain and expand it.

Come back to full consciousness in your body and offer your gratitude to God for the opportunity and gift you have just received, and be blissfully joyous. We love you most profoundly, and this love accompanies you each day of your life.

The Atomic Accelerator/Ascension Chair

A Tool for Creating a Chalice for Momentum of Light

Greetings, beloveds, this is Adama with Master Saint Germain.

I would like to talk to you about the atomic accelerator that many of you already know as the Ascension chair used on the inner planes for several purposes. Many of you have studied the teachings of the former dispensations with Master Saint Germain where this concept was first mentioned on many occasions, but it has not been fully understood. Allow us to give you greater understanding of this wondrous tool, beloved ones, so that you may use it to assist yourself and others on your pathway.

The energy of Master Saint Germain is here with me, and both of us together are now speaking to you, unifying our energies. In the light realms, there is such a unity of consciousness that we can mix our energies easily, and it gives us much joy.

The atomic accelerator is a gift to the Earth and to humanity from the heart of beloved Master Saint Germain. It is a tool to assist in raising the vibration of a candidate for Ascension. It contains the frequencies of pure Light of the Ascension Flame. It is used to raise one's vibration gradually and gently. When turned on full force, it can literally lift someone into the vibration of the electronic body for full, instant and permanent Ascension into the light realm and fifth dimensional consciousness.

In the past and now, many candidates on the inner planes, when ready for their earthly graduation, have received their full and majestic Ascension ceremony into the Light Realm, by sitting on one of these chairs; they are honored and supported by a large gathering of masters and beings from many dimensions. All energies remaining in the

197

records of the candidate that are less than pure Light and pure Love are dissolved in the intensity of the Ascension frequency. The candidate is instantly transformed and re-connected with the fullness of their Divine Essence and with all their spiritual gifts and attributes restored. This is the true and permanent ceremony of divine union, beloveds! This is the great alchemical marriage with Self that so many of you are longing for. Although this is not the only way one can make their Ascension—there are indeed several other options—this is the one most commonly used.

In order to receive this gift, one must be spiritually ready at all levels, or the results could be disastrous. You can trust that none of us would offer this blessing to anyone who has not yet attained the full level of initiations required. There are a few of these chairs on this planet in various spiritual, fifth dimensional retreats of the Great White Brotherhood. We have one in Telos and Saint Germain has his at Jackson Peak near Jackson Hole in Wyoming. There is also one in the Himalayas and in other retreats unknown to you.

Our channel Aurelia was directed by us several years ago to invite friends into her home once a month to conduct an Ascension ceremony ritual for those desiring to deepen their commitment to this goal, to the spiritual hierarchy of this planet and to their divine Presence. Each time Aurelia facilitated this ceremony with a group, a great number of us came to assist. Master Saint Germain always came with his portable atomic accelerator, which consists of a small etheric box that he positions under the chair in your dimension.

Each time, Master Saint Germain himself controls the intensity and velocity that each candidate can receive in order to raise their vibration to the next level, without significant discomfort or disturbance of the present level. The portable accelerator is designed for this purpose, and used for ceremonies performed in locations where surface people have chosen to do their Ascension work.

Aurelia has been conducting these Ascension ceremonies since 1994, when she lived in Montana. She has continued doing this service for the planet and for humanity ever since on a regular basis. She has performed this service of Light with every group that has come to Mount Shasta for initiatic journeys, and also in several other countries of the world during her travels abroad for conferences and workshops.

The Benefits and the Power of Building Momentum

We have noticed how wondrously powerful and beautiful the energies have increased over the years, more and more with each ritual Aurelia has facilitated. With each ceremony, the energies generated by the love and intention of the candidates have added and multiplied themselves to the sum total of all past ceremonies. With much interest and gratitude, we observe that, after many years of regular performance of this ritual, the Chalice of Light now created with each ceremony has built a huge momentum; it almost doubles in intensity and beauty each time this sacred ritual is performed. It is now affecting and helping not only the people participating in the group intention, but in creating a web of Light that touches almost the entire planet.

Many of you are not progressing on your spiritual journey as rapidly as you would like or achieving the results you want in your mundane endeavors mainly because you are not in the habit of creating enough momentum to attain your goals. Building greater momentum is what is needed to gather enough energy in your dimension to create whatever you want.

Even the beings embodying the "dark forces"
understand this principle very well, and are far
more persistent in building their momentum of
darkness than the People of Light have been
in building their momentum of Light.

The complacency that most of you practice has been one of the main contributing factors for the deep level of darkness, density and pain this entire planet has fallen into for so long. Those of us who have become masters have accumulated enough momentum of Light in order to manifest whatever we want, at any time we desire it. It is time that you wake up from your spiritual slumber.

Back in 1994, when Aurelia began to do her ceremonies with four or five people, the Chalice of Light created with each ceremony was quite small. As she continued to build her momentum year by year, the Chalice of Light has expanded exponentially.

With each ceremony created by intention, Master Saint Germain comes with his etheric atomic accelerator, invisible to those who are not yet clairvoyant, and puts it underneath the chair designated and decorated for that purpose. In our realm, we consider it to be a physical box, made of fifth dimensional technology with certain types of crystals. It has dials that one can turn on and off, like the technologies in your realm, except more advanced and evolved.

When the group is ready, and the invocation of intention is made by Aurelia, Master Saint Germain turns on the atomic accelerator. What does it do? All around and beneath the chair, there is an emanation of Ascension frequency that starts radiating outward. The person sitting on the chair receives most of it according to their level of evolution and capacity to receive.

The process has to be monitored because the Ascension Flame energy emanating from the accelerator could literally make you invisible and disappear quickly out of sight if it was turned on full. Be assured that until it is the right time for you to be raised into the full glory of the Ascension Flame, you will only receive increments each time you participate in one of these ceremonies.

As you evolve your consciousness, the Ascension Flame helps you to purify yourself more and more and assists in raising your vibration every time you set your intention through this sacred ritual.

It is so beautiful when you do this, if only you could see it from our perspective. As you gather together, you assist and hold the energy for each other. As each person comes forth to sit on the chair to declare their intention to ascend before their friends and before their God, and to do whatever it takes to make this happen, Master Saint Germain adjusts the dial of his accelerator to flood your forcefield with the level of Ascension frequency appropriate for you in the now moment.

Each time you speak from the heart on the chair and set your intention, you create an explosion of Love and Light that is most wondrous to behold. This is why, when you hold these gatherings, there is always a large assembly of Light Beings who come from the many realms of this planet, and other planets and star systems, who delight in observing what you are doing. They rejoice in witnessing this wondrous explosion of Light created by members of surface humanity. Each time, they bring you their love, support and comfort.

How to Create Your Ceremony

What you do is gather in a circle. Each person comes forth to sit on the designated Ascension Chair, and with a fully opened heart states their intention, preferably aloud, to manifest their goals for this life and for their Ascension. Make the most honorable prayer that your heart dictates or inspires you to do.

Each person holds in her/his hands a special crystal provided by the facilitator, and sits on the chair for about three to five minutes to perform their prayer. When finished, he/she gives a sign of completion with the eyes, and the group sings three "AUMs" to anchor the energy in the physical for the person sitting on the chair. Then the person returns to his/ her seat, and the next person in line takes her turn. People do not need to come in a specific order. There is always a flow that is created and each one takes his/her turn when they feel ready. The facilitator usually goes last, but this is not a rule.

When everyone is finished, Saint Germain and I, Adama, invite you to drink an elixir infused by us with the frequency of the "Golden Liquid Light."

The facilitator or assistant pours sparkling apple juice or some other juice into small containers and distributes it to each person present.

He/she then makes a short invocation to ask that this sparkling liquid that each one is holding be infused with the frequency of the Golden Liquid Light. Each person holds in his/her right hand the cup of juice *(or water if juice is not available)*. After the invocation the facilitator pauses for a moment for Saint Germain, myself and other presiding masters to charge the liquid at the frequency that is most appropriate for each person.

Then, when given the signal, each participant slowly drinks the liquid that is now a sacred elixir, expressing their deep gratitude to all involved for the rich blessing that is bestowed upon them.

This is just as powerful and effective as one of the elixirs from the inner plane. It has the same value. You have heard and read in one of our former books that when David Lloyd drank the elixir given to him by Master Saint Germain on Mount Shasta many years ago, he was lifted up; he totally disappeared and ascended in the Realms of Light creating much wonderment for his witness, Godfre Ray King.

Know, beloved ones, that David Lloyd could have made his Ascension differently, but it was his choice made in the inner plane to ascend in this particular manner, and it was granted. It happened because it was his time to ascend. We could charge the elixir for you in such a way that you would also disappear, but that's not the plan for right now. We are simply not going to do that, even if you ask! Not until it is your time, and believe us, several people have made that request. Sorry friends, but it is imperative that you wait for your right timing.

Know that there will come a time in the future when group Ascension will manifest, and in some cases, it will happen in front of others who will witness it. The time is not so far away, but you still have to wait a few more years. Know that this will never take anyone by surprise. If this happens to you, it is because you are totally prepared, and have fully consented to this type of Ascension.

When you hold your gatherings with the atomic accelerator, Master Saint Germain always controls the exact amount of energy given to each person, according to the level of vibration they can handle. We are not planning to have any of you disappearing prematurely!

Some of you are hesitant or shy to speak your heart openly in front of your brothers and sisters. Know, dear ones, in the light realms there are no secrets; everything is known. It is best that you start getting used to it now if you intend to come here. It will be easier later.

Once you make it to the higher dimensions nothing can be hidden. It is a very good practice to be able to open your heart in front of your brothers and sisters and hold nothing back. There is no shame in what you are doing! It is so beautiful! It creates an explosion of Light each time, and your Light is amplified as you support each other, building a Momentum of Light on your "journey to the stars."

We do invite you now to meet in groups of all sizes in your cities, villages and countries, at least once a month, as brothers and sisters, to reinforce your desires and intentions for your spiritual goals. Allow a momentum to build with each ceremony and with each participant's intentions.

Imagine how powerful this can be! What you will be doing is creating little webs of Ascension Light everywhere on the planet that will gain greater and greater momentum as more and more people do this. This Momentum of Light will increase in power as the created energies all join together.

This is the great Momentum of Light and Ascension Flame needed to propel this planet and all of humanity choosing to ascend in a great swirling tornado of Ascension Light. When you invoke Light, you assist darkness on the planet to dissolve, restoring every man, woman and child to the dignity of their divinity.

This is how darkness will be totally dispelled and swallowed up in a great victory of Light. But you have to do your part in your dimension, beloved children of our heart. It will not happen automatically without your contribution and participation, or just by wishing it.

In Telos, we enjoy your ceremonies of Love and Intention so very much. Be assured that we and Master Saint Germain also shall be with you every time, supporting and loving you all the way to your own victorious Ascension day.

Adama - Do you want to comment or do you have any questions on this?

Aurelia - This is a most incredible offering that you have given us about getting groups together around the world, and experiencing levels of Ascension frequency through our creations of Ascension ceremonies and taking in spiritual elixirs. You are offering us a permanent increase of frequency through this beautiful ritual, is that correct?

Adama - We do, and you can do it as often as you wish. It is up to you if you want to use this as a tool to assist yourself on your pathway. It is a tool whose energies simply build up more and more as you unite together. Many people want to ascend, but they often forget to set their intention and are not always willing to put in the effort necessary to attain the fullness of their spiritual freedom.

When you get together and reinforce your intentions, it becomes more powerful in your life. These gatherings can be created as wonderful ways to spend time together with like-minded people. You can even share a meal together afterwards, if you wish. This is the Lemurian way, to do things together, without pomp or circumstance, by simply being the gods and goddesses that we are. We invite you to do and be the same. Take advantage of the tools that will help you raise your consciousness in simple and pleasant ways.

And so be it, beloved children of our heart. Be in peace and in love with yourself. Soon, we will meet with you in the arms of Love.

For your information, Mount Shasta Light Publishing has created a booklet with more details about this Ascension ceremony. It is now available for purchase on our web site www.mslpublishing.com for those desiring to facilitate this kind of activity in your area. The Ascension Flame of Purification and Immortality *is available in English and Spanish. Eventually it will be in other languages.*

Knowing the supreme glory of that hour,
I can but urge each dear child of God
To prepare for that glorious moment!
When the hour comes and the summons
From the Father of Light reaches your heart,
You will also know the full and true purpose
For human incarnations.
- Lord Sananda

Chapter Sixteen

The Flame of Resurrection, A Sixth Ray Activity

With a Meditation to the Temple of Resurrection

Adama with Jesus/Sananda and Nada

Group - What is Adama planning for us tonight?

Aurelia - *I had a talk with Adama this afternoon, as I did not have any idea what we were going to talk about this evening. Adama would like to talk about the Resurrection Flame and the healing attributes of this Flame. This wondrous Flame is not well known to the majority of the people on this dimension, even for those who know about it. They usually don't understand how to use it. The Resurrection Flame is one of the seven major Flames of God that have been available to people on this planet since the beginning of time. It has an action of its own, but also carries another aspect of healing.*

The whole world is in desperate need of many kinds and levels of healing at this time. The word healing has a broad meaning, including many aspects and many levels. Before we can be whole and express the fullness of the Light of the "I AM" again, we have to heal all aspects of ourselves on deeper and deeper levels, until completion. You know, people have heard much about healing in so many different ways on the third dimension, but true healing is little understood.

In fact, in order to understand true healing, it would be wise to understand in greater measure the attributes of the seven major Flames of God constantly flooding this planet to nurture, recharge and sustain life.

The understanding that Adama would like to convey this evening is healing on a higher level, a true healing, not just a temporary solution which requires a more permanent resolution at a later time. The Flame of Resurrection is another extraordinary tool among others, which is free, easy to use and very effective. Unfortunately, it has been forgotten and so is not used by the majority of the people.

The emerald green vibration of the Fifth Ray of Healing and the energies of the Great Jade Temple is one tool, but there are many more awe-inspiring ones. The more aware we become of the tools we have at our disposal at any time, and the more we use them, the more we can transform our lives with ease and grace. Now Adama would like to give us a greater understanding of The Resurrection Flame. He will also discuss electrons, and how we can raise our consciousness by using the seven sacred Flames of God and the right use of electrons. The Flame of Resurrection prepares us at the soul level and prepares our bodies for physical immortality, if this is what is chosen. It is also a Flame that prepares you to receive the full transformation of the Ascension Flame.

Let me explain the term "Flames." On this planet, the Seven Sacred Flames are the main ones who have sustained humanity in its evolution and life. Of course, in higher dimensions, there are many more, and we are now embracing the energies of the twelve Flames. This means five more Flames are more available to us as we raise our consciousness out of the spiritual slumber we have been in for so long. Indeed, there are hundreds more of them which are not revealed in our dimension. For now, let us rest ourselves in this marvelous one this evening. Because they are so wondrous, we could talk about each one for hours and perhaps days.

There are in Creation many different attributes of God, and each one is represented by its own energetic vibration and action that we call "Flames" or "Rays." They are also called by other names as well. However, their names are not as important as understanding their usage and influence in our lives. The main seven Flames are also known as the Rainbow Rays and they are connected to everything in Creation.

There are seven days of the week, seven notes on the musical octave, seven main chakras, seven main endocrine glands, and seven main organs and systems in the body, etc. The list is quite long. Each one of these Rays represents a specific color vibration and is connected with one of the systems I mentioned above. For example, each day of the week is amplified with the energies of one of the Rays and its corresponding color vibration. Each note on the musical octave represents a specific color and Ray energy. Each one of the seven glands and the seven main organs in your body, each one of the seven main chakras, is connected to one of the Rays or Flames and the energy with which it is connected is amplified in that area, or day, etc.

The Resurrection Flame also carries the energy of transformation to assist us to move into the fifth dimension awareness. On the etheric plane and on all dimensions, beautiful temples are erected to amplify each one of the many Flames or attributes of the Creator. There are many temples in Telos to nurture these Flames, and hundreds of temples existed in the time of Lemuria for that very purpose. The Flame of Resurrection is something you can use forever, through eternity, always gaining from it.

I now bring Adama.

$\mathcal{A}dama$ - Greetings my dearest ones, this is your friend and mentor Adama. It is such a pleasure for me and for my team to be with you once more today to present pearls of wisdom and knowledge to those who want to expand their awareness and understanding of God in all its wondrous attributes. I am here today with the guardians of the Flame of Resurrection, Lord Jesus/Sananda with his beloved twin flame Nada, who was also known in your world as Mary Magdalene in her last incarnation, 2,000 years ago. They are here to beam the radiance of their Love to all of you.

You have been taught so little of the real truth about God and your divinity in your short incarnation on this planet so far. Your knowledge of God is so limited to understand the mysteries of Life. There is much knowledge at your disposal today to be embraced and understood for the unfoldment of your consciousness and your reconnection with all aspects of your divinity so that you can attain finally your spiritual freedom.

Nearly all of you have experienced thousands of incarnations on this planet, and for most in the current incarnation, you've been presented with very few pearls of true knowledge. As all this is now changing, tonight we will impart to your awareness another one of these spiritual treasures, another tool to assist you in your transition to spiritual Oneness and wholeness.

The Flame of Resurrection in its vibration and action is not uniquely a healing Flame; its sphere of action is vast, and in this short time together, we can cover only the basics. Its actions are of universal dimension, and take place at many levels and frequencies. 2,000 years ago, the Master Jesus used the Flame of Resurrection to resurrect his own body in the tomb after the death of his mortal body. This alone should give you a clue of the wonders of that Flame. When contemplating its greater meaning, what does resurrection really mean? What it did for this great Avatar 2,000 years ago, it could also do for you right now. The attributes of this Flame have not diminished; on the contrary, it has gathered much momentum and its powers have multiplied many times.

Lord Jesus/Sananda, with his beloved twin flame Nada, are

together the Chohans or guardians of this Sacred Flame. They are both high-level ascended beings, and they are ever so willing to assist you at any time, especially with the wonders of this Sacred Flame. Also, note that around the time of Easter is when this Flame is most active on this planet. This time of the year is a window of opportunity to infuse your entire consciousness, being and world with this wondrous Flame. It is also when nature is infused by the Resurrection Flame in greater measure and becomes alive again.

Although this Flame is active at all times, Easter is when its energy doubles in intensity for the benefit of mankind, in commemoration of the Christ energies brought back to this planet by Lord Jesus/Sananda. The Flame of Resurrection, as a Sixth Ray activity, also embodies the energies of Selfless Service and Ministration. That is what Jesus embodied and demonstrated by his life and his selfless service. He has remained in service to the planet and all of mankind until this present time, and will continue through millennia to come.

His experience with the Flame of Resurrection wasn't unique to him; he simply knew how to use these life-giving and life-enhancing energies. Now that you have all evolved yourselves to a greater level of understanding, it is time for you to use this for yourself. It is so wondrous, and I am so happy to bring you this knowledge. There are many tools at your disposal to create ease in your life and to accelerate your transformation and your evolutionary path. You simply need to be aware of them and use them diligently in your daily life.

When you desire healing in your body, you need the energy of the Resurrection Flame to accomplish this by taking into your body a much higher frequency than you already carry. A superficial, temporary healing is not what you are striving for; you all seek something that is permanent and uplifting. You want healing that will reconnect you more consciously with the divine being that you are, which, in truth, is the source of everything you ever want and desire. You want your healing to reflect and embody once again your divinity, your very prime nature. It is your birthright as a child of God.

When the master Jesus said, "I AM the Resurrection and the Life," he was not talking about his human self in incarnation. He was teaching the divine law of the great "I AM" that lives in the Sacred Heart of all of you, your divine Self, not yet fully expressed in your present state of awareness. He expressed it because he was fully connected to his Divine Essence. Understand that the Resurrection Flame is an energy you can easily use for your benefit by focusing on it, invoking it, and beginning to play with it. Be creative!

Group - It sounds pretty awesome to us. Until Aurelia mentioned it, we had never heard of it. How can we actually use this and make it work in our lives?

Adama - It is one of the many attributes of God. You can resurrect your finances, you can resurrect your bodies, you can resurrect family harmony, and you can resurrect a great number of things you want to expand in your life. The resurrection energies are not limited in any way whatsoever.

You can use the words "I AM," knowing that it is the unlimited aspect of you, or you could say something like, "From the Lord God of my being, I call forth now to receive a great infusion of Resurrection Flame in every cell, atom, and electron in my physical body, my emotional body and all my subtle bodies. I wish to heal and resurrect all aspects of my life. *(Name other things you personally want to resurrect such as finances, talents, memories, harmony, etc.)*" The sky is not even the limit in using this powerful energy. If you experience lack of any kind in your life, if your body is not yet in a state of luminosity and immortality, if you are not yet manifesting absolute divine beauty, youth and perfection, it means that the electrons composing your physical structure are still suffering levels of distortions. Call the Resurrection Flame to come to your rescue and assist you.

Group - *How often do we need to do this?*

Adama - In your dimension, because energy moves so slowly in comparison to the fifth, where creation is instant, you must focus on what you want to create until it manifests in order to obtain results. You also need to add the focus of your loving emotions into the object of your creation. If you focus only once, your chances of manifesting what you want are rather slim. It is not a question of repeating affirmations like a parrot, but of sending your loving thoughts throughout the day as you go about your business, with the absolute knowingness that your creation is manifesting through your love and intention.

If you also choose to do affirmations, which are very helpful, be sure that you repeat them, not as a supplication, but as a statement of loving intention, with the full intensity of emotion from your heart, infusing the object of your desire with as much faith and gratitude as possible.

It is always helpful to visualize the Resurrection Flame as a golden orange-yellow energy, luminescent in color like you see when you watch a summer sunset. Make it real. Give it life in your heart and mind, because as you visualize it, so it becomes. If you want healing, infuse the problem you want to heal with that wondrous energy, and be sure to sustain it long enough to get results.

Group - *Could you give us a brief description on the Seven Flames and their attributes?*

Adama - The *Flame of Wisdom and Illumination* resonates to various tones of yellow. The *Flame of Love* resonates to various tones of pink-red and ruby. The *Flame of the Will of God* resonates to various tones of blue. The *Flame of Healing* resonates to the tones of emerald green and its many variations. The *Flame of Ascension* is pure white and encompasses all other Flames in its vibration. The *Resurrection Flame* is our focus today. Last but not least, most of you already know about the *Violet Transmuting Flame* brought back to Earth at the beginning of the last century, as a great dispensation, by our beloved Saint Germain.

The energies of the Flames are connected to each of your chakras. As you evolve your consciousness, you will discover many more chakras that will be activated. The Flames work individually and together in a synchronistic way like rainbows of light to assist and sustain you. You will discover a great many more, such as the Flame of Joy, the Flame of Harmony, the Flame of Comfort and Peace, etc. It is simply endless.

***What I would like to express or explain next
is a basic understanding of electrons.***

The smallest manifestation of life can be measured in terms which men would understand as electrons. These electrons represent particles of energy from the body of Prime Creator, which is eternally self-sustaining, indestructible, self-luminous and intelligent. Electrons are pure universal light substance, responding like lightning to the creative powers of both God and men. In varying forms, they make up the atoms of the physical world. Interstellar space is filled with this pure "light-essence." The number of electrons, which combine with each other in a specific atom, is the result of, and determined by, conscious "thought." The rate at which they whirl around the central core is the result of, and determined by, "feelings." The intensity of the whirling motion within the central core is the "breath of God." Therefore, the most concentrated activity of "Divine Love," whatever energy grows your food, whatever substance you find in the third dimension, is all made of various manifestations of electrons that have been qualified differently. Everything is made of the same "stuff" called electrons. There are those who use other names; it doesn't matter what name you choose to give it. It is all made of the same thing, prime Source energy as "Love."

Electrons are created as energy particles from ethereal planes of consciousness; this energy is neutral and totally at the service of Life. They manifest in form only when they become qualified by other conscious parts of life. Electrons take various forms, shapes and densities according to how they are qualified. In your world, when you qualify energy with less than pure Love, when you create with anger, fear or greed, you are misusing electrons and creating distortions in their original purpose of serving Life. This miscreation then become yours to own. You have to live and experience the programming you have qualified them with, until you eventually balance your debts to life with Love, thus purifying the electrons you have misused. This is what you have called the "working out or balancing of karma."

Take good note, my dear brothers and sisters, of what I am going to say next. This is most important for you to always remember.

God gives you, on a daily basis, an unlimited number of electrons to create your life with, and you are always free to create it in any way you choose. According to what you create with your thoughts, intentions and emotions, your life always reflects how you use the electrons. In general, humanity has not understood the right use of electrons, or in other words, the right use of the energy at their disposal. It is knowledge that has been forgotten. By misusing energy as you do on the surface of the Earth, you have created much pain and difficulty for yourself, for your families, for your planet and for everyone evolving here.

Group - Do we misqualify the use of that energy through self-doubt, judgment, fear and all aspects of our emotions and actions that do not express love?

Adama - Yes, electrons want to respond to Love. When you misqualify them with vibrations other than Love or Joy, they become distorted in various ways, and that distortion becomes your cosmic responsibility. How do you think the electrons used for nuclear energy or other types of destruction feel? Remember, they carry prime Creator consciousness and intelligence. Because they are commissioned to serve Life unconditionally, they have to serve mankind in whatever way mankind chooses to use them. These electrons, more often than not, remain embedded in the negativity of mankind, sometimes for eons. This is not what they want or what they have been created for, but they must submit to your choices.

Mankind can use electrons to create an absolute paradise for themselves, for the planet and for everything around them, or they can use them to destroy their world. This is the experiment of free will on this planet. Not all planets have free will to the extent you have on Earth. The misuse of free will has been a very painful experience for humanity over eons of time. This is why it is so important to understand the right and the wrong use of electrons. The Resurrection Flame can help you purify the electrons you have misused back into harmony. All the Flames of God are made of electrons, as is everything else.

Group - *You are saying that if we act out of fear or any negative emotions, the energy is misused or distorted. From Creator Source, electrons are imbued with Love and alive with consciousness, flowing to and through us for our use.*

Adama - Exactly, and this is constant everywhere in the Universe. Electrons represent the energy you use to create your daily life. If you misuse electrons or energy, it creates fields of darkness around and inside of you. If you misuse these to create fear within yourself or project this kind of energy onto others, through doubt and judgment, the electrons of your own body become distorted. They eventually create disease, illness, lack of vitality, aging, etc.

Group - *How does using the Resurrection Flame correspond to our needs, as we are moving into mastery, gaining the wisdom and understanding from our experiences?*

Adama - First of all, you need to understand that the Resurrection Flame is not the only Flame nurturing Life; all Flames do. Be aware that you cannot freely misuse God's energy without consequences. When you qualify God's energy with fear and resentment, the electrons flow discordantly. When you qualify God's energy with Love, the electrons flow harmoniously, because that is their nature. Your nature is divine, as is theirs.

Group - *We have carried for many lifetimes patterns of abandonment, betrayal and rejection. How would one use the Resurrection Flame to begin working with such deep-seated aspects of Self?*

Adama - First, you have to work with your emotions and become aware of your thought patterns. You can invoke the Flame of Resurrection to assist you in restoring harmony in your life and to heal all your issues. When you begin to re-qualify energy or electrons with the Flames of God, the electrons start spinning in a different direction, clockwise instead of counterclockwise. You can use the Flame of Resurrection consciously for cleansing and for raising the vibration in all your body systems, such as your emotional body, your physical body and your mental body, above the vibrations of distortion, disease and lack.

This inner work needs to be embraced as a way of life, as an unfolding process, "progress in action," not something you do only once in a while. It is the most important work you can take on in your life. It is the key to the spiritual freedom you so much yearn for. You can work with the Resurrection Flame for a lifetime and it will always ease your way and create more wonders in your life.

Now how many people use the old sentence, as given by the

Master Jesus 2,000 years ago, "I am the Resurrection and the Life"? This was a mantra that was given to him by his teacher the Great Divine Director when he was traveling in India during the years previous to his public ministry. Understand that he actively used the Flame of Resurrection during the course of his life to such an extent and with such a momentum, that after his physical death, he had accumulated enough energy in his causal body to raise his physical body from the dead. It was from that mantra alone that he succeeded in building his momentum.

He also drew from the pool of reserves of that energy he had garnered unto himself to perform many of the miracles you are familiar with, and those that were not recorded at the time. One of his assignments was to fully embody the Resurrection Flame and become it, in order to accomplish whatever he wanted. And this he did with grace and with the fullness of His heart. What worked for him 2,000 years ago will work equally for you now.

Group - *Wow, Adama!*

Adama - This is the kind of thing you can do quite easily, and there is no financial drain involved. The gifts of this Flame are impersonal, not limited to one being 2,000 years ago, but to all of the children of the Creator at any time, anywhere. Some people use it for their finances: "I am the resurrection and the life of my finances." When you start using it, many things will be revealed to your awareness for your spiritual growth. Before you can receive what you want, you may have to do some housecleaning or corrections in your consciousness. As you focus on the object of your desires, what is out of alignment will be shown to you, and as you change your consciousness, your life will also change for the better.

Your "GodSelf" will bring forth into your conscious awareness the erroneous beliefs and attitudes that stand in the way of your manifestations. They will be shown to you for your consideration and learning of a greater wisdom. It is up to each person to develop the discernment to recognize, acknowledge them and make the necessary changes in your consciousness. If you become aware of the misuse of finances from the past, start using the Violet Flame of Transmutation and the Flame of Forgiveness from the heart of the Mother Quan Yin, along with the Resurrection energy to assist you to clear those energies of the past, and to contemplate what you are learning from it.

The Resurrection Flame has the tone and color that can assist you. Visualize it like radiant golden sun-type energy, more orange than gold. See yourself sitting in a seat totally engulfed in the Resurrection Flame energy, as you do your spiritual work with this vibration.

You know, old age and degeneration have never been natural attributes of life. The appearance of your physical body is determined by the amount of light that is carried within your lower vehicles, the emotional, mental, etheric and physical bodies. The natural emanation of light through these body systems forms the protective wall referred to as the tube of light around you. When the electrons move slowly in their particular organs and cells, they draw less light from your Higher Self, building a natural resistance, which causes the light stream to grow weaker. How much vitality you are going to have in your body and how you are feeling has to do with how fast the electrons can spin in your body.

The more toxins you have and the less light you hold, the slower the electrons spin which encourages old age, disease, misalignment and malfunction of the organs, glands and systems. Eventually your whole body experiences aging. In Telos, we have attained immortality because we have learned to keep ourselves and everything we do in our lives, our mental attitudes and our emotional bodies clear of negativity. We clear ourselves regularly with the many tools we are providing you through our teachings. Our electrons are spinning at the speed that keeps our bodies always young and beautiful. Immortality is not such a mystery once you understand it, but the unfoldment of "real Life" that is divine and natural.

Group - Do masters ever make mistakes?

Adama - You have to realize that when you talk about masters and mastery, there are various levels. There are masters of the fourth dimension, masters of the fifth dimension and masters of all dimensions. In each dimension, one learns greater and greater levels of mastery. For example, if you refer to masters in the fourth dimension, they can make mistakes, but it is also their learning process, as it is for all of you. You learn primarily by your mistakes. The mistakes they make are not very serious, as they work within much greater wisdom and under the guidance of masters of the higher dimensions.

In the higher realms, we work in groups and unity, so we always get the benefit of the wisdom of the whole and of those who have a greater spiritual attainment. Unlike in your dimension, no one has to work alone and take on big responsibilities on their own. These are the wondrous benefits of surrender to a spiritual hierarchy made of Masters embodying greater Love and Wisdom in each dimension above the one in which we presently dwell. Decisions are always made for the benefit of the whole and to implement the Will of the Creator.

You are never judged for your mistakes, but you judge yourselves. Some people have so much resistance to learning the concepts of divine law that they often choose, at a soul level, to develop a cancer situation and die from it in order to learn their wisdom. On the other hand, if someone decides *(always at a soul level)* to develop the same type of cancer in order to heal themselves and learn their lessons from it in this life, they can heal themselves easily and naturally. They may start changing their diet or their attitude towards life and others. They may begin to feel grateful for everything in their life experience and cultivate joy and forgiveness. As they do this with a sense of renewal and self-love, true healing takes place. Anything can be healed, anything!

Whatever happens in your life, let's say that you lose your house in a fire, or are in an accident and lose a leg, or become blind, or lose large sums of money or suffer a broken relationship—no matter what happens, whether the challenge is small or large, instead of being angry, depressed and bitter, say to yourself "What can I learn and how can I heal from this?"

Surrendering to the lessons you need to learn is the key to walking through them quickly. Your life will then change, and you will not have to grapple the rest of your life with the same lessons. You can move on to new experiences that bring you more joy. Lessons don't always have to be difficult to learn; they become difficult for those who have chosen again and again through many incarnations to totally ignore them.

There are those who have had lifetime after lifetime of not wanting to see, to know or to have anything to do with their lessons.

There comes a time when life will no longer allow you to ignore the promptings of your soul, and this is when life can, for a while, become quite difficult. It is not required that you grapple with your lessons forever. You can move through them quickly, and begin to outpicture the beautiful diamond light that you are, on the way to your enlightenment. The lessons you are learning manifest because "you" have created them in the first place. It is not that God sends you lessons to annoy you. Through the right use or misuse of "free will," you have consciously or unconsciously created your reality.

As you take responsibility, look at your lessons and say, "What is it that I need to learn out of this mess I have created, and what blessings are in it? What is the gift?" Know that any negative or difficult situation you experience in life can be turned into something very, very wonderful, if it is approached the right way. Even a disease or a financial loss can open the opportunity for much greater blessings to manifest once you open your consciousness to receive them. How many people gain great wisdom from their illnesses or a relationship that has ended?

For example, there are still a great number of people mistreating animals in your society because in their consciousness, they are so far removed from the truth of their divinity and the Oneness of all life. Many still live in the illusion that animals are a lower form of life, and therefore less valuable than people, right? The way you treat so many of your animals, inflicting experiences of slaughter, abandonment, caging, chaining, lab experimentations, etc. on their souls does not reflect the qualities of an enlightened society. Civilizations who treat their animals the way so many people still do on this planet are considered primitive.

When people mistreat or hurt animals, they deny that animals are made of the same "stuff," electrons, from prime Creator as they are. It is the same energy your body is made of, your table, your chairs and your computer. Once you fully realize that everything that exists is of God's energy, and primal energy is all the same, you become fully aware that you can "never" hurt any part of life without hurting yourself equally.

When harming yourself or any part of life, your actions become your own creation, and the energies used for that creation generate fields of darkness around you that at some point will have to be purified by you. This is what comes back in your life as challenges or karma for your consideration. Whenever you hurt one part of life, it doesn't matter what it is, you are hurting yourself even more. Once humanity understands this principle and stops creating in separation, creating with Love can begin, and everything will return to its original divine perfection.

Group - Let me also add, Adama, it is not just the animal kingdom, but also the plant and the mineral kingdoms, the nature spirits and the elementals that suffer at the hands of unenlightened people. So many facets of society rape and pillage the Earth, and because of this, we are no longer operating under the laws of divine grace.

Adama - Oh, of course. I only use the animals as one example. Do those polluting and raping the planet think they are not accountable for their actions, and do they think their behavior is without consequence in their evolution? The ones poisoning your planet, polluting your waterways, polluting the air, and the ones creating chemtrails in the sky to consciously poison your very breath of life will suffer the return of their own creations. No one, and I mean no one, can ever escape the great law of divine justice.

As you sow, so shall you reap! Some beings on Earth at this time have done and still do so much harm to the planet and to their human brothers and sisters, that it will take a great number of lifetimes of hardship and learning their lessons of Love to mend their ways and make up, in dedicated service to Life, for all the harm and pain they have created.

Group - It is fairly safe to assume that people like that won't be ascending into the fifth dimension any time soon.

Adama - They certainly will not. Not everyone will experience the fifth dimension consciousness by 2012 through the Ascension process. That date is only for those who are diligently making themselves ready. The rest of humanity will be held back until every requirement needed to receive such a divine grace has been fulfilled. It is expected that some will make it before 2012, and others will ascend with the planet. Some souls will remain in the third and/or fourth dimension as long as needed to "graduate" to this level, even if it takes them 20, 30 to 40 years or longer. You have all of eternity, and no one is going to force you into anything.

Group - Another rumor floating around on the surface is that everyone is going to make it into the fifth dimension as the Earth shifts into the Ascension mode.

Adama - Everyone who has shifted their consciousness to unconditional love and has diligently fulfilled all other requirements for Ascension will certainly make it along with the planet. However, there are others who will have to experience their creation and continue their evolution until they "get it," and shift to Love and unity consciousness. Much assistance and mercy will be granted to those choosing Ascension at this time. Those not fervently choosing this will not make it in this cycle. Basically, most people on the planet are good-hearted and loving, even if they are not yet spiritually awakened.

There are those, as well, who have repeatedly created so many problems on this planet and inflicted so much pain on others, that even if they choose to align with the Christ consciousness now, they are going to have to face and experience the return of their miscreation. For them, the Ascension becomes a possibility in another cycle. Actually, everyone will eventually ascend back to the Heart of the Creator; it is simply a question of time. It will happen for them when they choose to do their spiritual work and make the necessary changes in their consciousness.

There are other third dimensional planets in other universes where these souls will be admitted to learn their lessons and continue their evolution according to their choices and level of willingness to make changes.

No one is exempt from facing their miscreation and having to balance everything back to Love. The fifth dimension is a place of Purity, Love and Divine Perfection. Do you think that the gates of the fifth dimension will open to anyone who tries to enter with their baggage of karma, negativity, violence and darkness? Absolutely not. It would pollute and create serious rifts in the fifth dimension. That is exactly what you're trying to get away from.

Everyone will have an opportunity to ascend into the fifth dimension who so chooses. The doors of opportunity for Ascension are open, but realize that there are many who will make other choices, and those choices are honored and respected. When they feel they have sufficiently experienced rounds of birth and rebirth and cycles of reincarnation, pain and suffering, they will make another choice. They will change and they will eventually come back into alignment, because they are part of the divine plan and also part of God.

I invite everyone to make this choice in your heart. Do you want to come now or do you want to wait for another long cycle?

Because the corridors of Ascension are opening wide at this time, it doesn't mean they will remain open forever. The corridors of Ascension have been closed for a long time to surface dwellers on this planet, and no one knows when they will close or open again. This decision is not within our jurisdiction. We can't tell you what we don't know, but we know that the window of opportunity is wide open now, and it could be another several thousand to several hundred thousand years before there is another such opportunity again. We urge you to get off the picket fence of indecision. Make a choice in your heart about whether you want to come now or later, and be committed to your choice.

For those who are truly making this choice to come now, let me clarify something. Some on the Earth right now, because of their advanced age, such as your senior citizens, have made the choice to come into Ascension on the inner plane, but will not qualify for full ascension in this lifetime, because there is too much for them yet to clear and to understand. It would be too difficult for them. Some have old, sick bodies and have not yet had the opportunity to open fully to this understanding. At a soul level, they are good people and they have not done any harm. Many of them will leave the body, but this doesn't mean they are not coming into the Ascension. Their divine grace is that they will be given another opportunity for incarnation in the "new world" we are moving into, and the process of ascension in the next life will be much easier and joyful for them.

Group - Are those who will be incarnating on the new planet called Excelsior to finish their work there before moving back into fifth dimensional Earth?

Adama - Some will incarnate on Excelsior or elsewhere, while others will incarnate back here, because the incarnation cycle on Earth is not over. It really does not matter, because this wondrous little planet, Excelsior, has much to offer to assist the healing of souls who have been in pain on Earth for so long. Those who incarnate on Excelsior will ascend from there and meet with all of us here, because it is all part of the same great Ascension plan.

As people on this planet are moving into fourth and fifth dimensional consciousness, they will continue to give birth to children. Most civilizations in the higher dimensions have children, in one way or another. Many of these souls will ascend physically the next time, as they have already made the choice to come into Ascension in their next life experience. The right opportunity will be at hand for every soul. Those who incarnate on Excelsior will definitely have a golden opportunity there, as wondrous as those who will return here for incarnation. Excelsior is a wondrous and beautiful little planet, very similar to Earth, which has not yet known any negativity. Excelsior can be compared to Lemuria, the garden of Eden, the wondrous and gracious way it used to be in Her early time before the fall of consciousness. Many souls from here have been incarnating on Excelsior in the last 20 to 25 years and are very much enjoying their new abode.

I would like to expand more on the use of the Resurrection Flame to rejuvenate the physical body. I also want to touch on immortality, a vast subject. Before talking about immortality, it is important that you understand the use of the Resurrection Flame. The Resurrection energy is a key vibration for attaining immortality of the physical body. If you want to shift the body, right now, without going through the process of physical death, the Resurrection Flame will greatly assist you.

When you take a real interest in your own evolution and allow the Resurrection Flame to pass through your body regularly, you embody greater harmony, beauty and vitality. Immortality then begins to express more tangibly within your life stream and you begin to feel the rejuvenation taking place.

The soul that has attained a certain level of maturity should be more beautiful and exquisite in face and form as the years pass. The aging process that you presently experience is gradually going to change in the years to come. It is already changing for many. You will soon begin to express more beauty and perfection in your physical body as you age. You will feel more alive and begin to experience limitlessness. Does this make your heart sing?

Distortions in the body, loss of vitality, illnesses and looking older is not a divine attribute. We would like to encourage you to understand that the Flame of Resurrection has the ability to reverse aging and to make you glow. Can you imagine? If every cell, atom and electron in your body were to glow with the Flame of Resurrection, you would become luminous and radiant. Your bodies would take the form of the exquisite beauty of your divine Self. As you age, you would become more exquisitely beautiful and divine in your physical form. This is what we have attained in Telos. Since we are all the same genetically, what we have attained, all of you can attain as well. Are you ready for the meditation?

Meditation

Journey to the Temple of Resurrection in the Fifth Dimension

Adama with Sananda and Nada

We now invite all of you to take a journey in consciousness to a wondrous temple in the fifth dimension called the
Temple of Resurrection. It is a vast temple like all the fifth
dimensional temples. One of the functions of this temple is
to assist humanity with the energies of true resurrection,
which takes place at many levels.

In your immediate and future evolution you are no longer
looking to simply manifest superficial or temporary healings
for all the different problems that burden you, whether they
are physical, emotional, mental or spiritual. What you really
want to do is to infuse this energy in your body and your
consciousness, knowing that it will assist in raising your
vibrational frequency above your present life circumstances.
The Flame of Resurrection is always available to you at any
time and it doesn't cost anything. All it takes is a bit of your
time, your focus and your love as you invoke it forth and
work with it.

Now connect to your "I AM Presence" in your heart as you
take several deep breaths. Ask your light body to descend
over you and take you in consciousness to the Resurrection
Temple; it knows very well how to get you there. If you wish
to come along with us on that journey, I invite you to formu-
late your intent in your heart now. *(Pause)*

This vast etheric temple is glowing as a golden sun from a
distance, with vapors of golden sunlight all around it. See
a golden crystalline sun-like substance, more orange than
gold, manifesting as walls and floors. In various places,

it reflects the luminosity of other Flames and other color vibrations. Your Divine Essence takes you there in your light body and you are becoming more aware of this place in your consciousness.

Now see yourself entering a big hall, called "The Hall of Resurrection." It contains many facets, many doorways and many chambers. Many beings from different dimensions are using this hall as well, which vibrates at a very high frequency. See a group of beings, guardians of the temple, approaching you to welcome and accompany you in your journey here.

People of the third dimension are taken into chambers designed for their level of evolution and frequency tolerance. This temple is well attended, as many souls from this whole galaxy and beyond who assist the lower realms come here daily to recharge and to be uplifted. Breathe in this wonderful golden Flame energy and let it infuse every particle of your being. *(Pause)*

This Flame will assist the expansion of your consciousness, your understanding of life and evolution to a greater level than the one you presently hold. Breathe in and integrate the consciousness, the energy of the Resurrection. Breathe it into every cell, atom and electron of your physical body. As you use the Resurrection Flame on a regular basis, it will continue to expand within you, unto eternity. Beings of higher dimensions still use it to expand their consciousness to higher and higher levels, to resurrect and embrace more and more of their divinity. The possibilities of Resurrection are simply endless.

Stay with us for a time in the Hall of Resurrection and with those of the temple who have graciously volunteered to accompany you. Millions of the Resurrection Flame angels nurture and minister to humanity each day, especially those who make a conscious effort to contact them. You have access not only to the Flame, but also to all the wonderful angels willing to work with you on a one-to-one basis, to nurture and to love you back to your spiritual freedom.

As you stand in this wondrous golden hall, you will see countless golden Flames of Resurrection burning in all shapes and sizes to assist the Earth and evolving humanity. They burn perpetually, as another aspect of the "eternal unfed Flame of Life" of Creator Source. They assist all life and the planet not only in the third dimension, but also in all dimensions inside and out of the Earth, the galaxies and the universe.

As you walk into the hall and gaze at all the wonders you perceive, you come to a specific circle reserved for Earth's surface dwellers. The circle consists of Flames of various sizes and shapes that look somewhat like different varieties of flowers. There are Resurrection seats, inviting souls visiting the temple to sit and to soak quietly in the energy. Now choose one of the seats and make yourself comfortable. Simply sit on the one calling you, looking like a lotus flower, but it is a lotus flame. This golden lotus flame enfolds your body completely to raise your energies. As you sit and contemplate the wonders of your experience, continue to breathe in the energy to absorb all you can. Feel the flame permeating every aspect of your being.

Take a few minutes to consciously request what you would like to clear and what areas in your life you would most like to resurrect. Keep focusing on the great gift you are receiving, being nurtured and loved by the angels that are accompanying you and attending your needs. Keep breathing, because you want to take as much as possible of this energy back with you, into your physical body. The more you take in, the more you are raising your vibration.

Feel your body being imprinted with the Resurrection energy; become aware of how it feels and how the flame is affecting you. Awaken to its sensation and allow your sensory bodies to open to feel more of all aspects of Life. Feel the joy that it brings to your heart. Absorb all you can and feel how much lighter you are now becoming. It is as if the angels are carrying you. Consciously set your intention to raise your vibration with this wonderful flame that can lift you up and out of many of the predicaments you are trying to heal and balance.

Don't hesitate to invite the Master Jesus/Sananda with his beloved Nada to assist you with their momentum of the Resurrection Flame. They are masters of that Flame. If Sananda as Jesus could raise his own body after the crucifixion and use the same energy to raise Lazarus from the dead, he can certainly assist you in great measure. What he did, you can also do, but you must build your own momentum over a period of time as he did. You can use this Flame to literally resurrect your body into a divine state of perfection, beauty, radiance, luminosity, immortality and limitlessness.

When you feel complete, get up from your seat, and return to meet us at the entrance of the Hall of Resurrection. When ready, return to full consciousness in your body on the Earth and take this energy back with you. Know that you are most welcome to return to the Resurrection Temple any time and receive all the benefits. You may go every day, or as often as you please. In your heart, express your deep gratitude for the blessings you just received and thank those who have assisted your visit to the Resurrection Temple.

The Elixirs of Immortality come from the Resurrection Flame.

We now send you love, peace, harmony and healing from Telos and from the members of our community of Light. Know that we are with you at all times and we are as close to you as your call. Any time you want to connect with us, our hearts are open. We are your brothers and sisters, and we love you very much. And so be it.

Aurelia - Thank you so much, Adama, for this wonderful, wonderful message and meditation and for introducing us to the Resurrection Flame and its many attributes for our lives. What a wonderful gift and what a blessing! We express our heartfelt gratitude to Nada and Sananda for your presence and the contribution of your love and radiance here today. We love you so much, Adama, Sananda and Nada. Thank you for being the wonderful teachers that you are.

Adama - It has been our delight and great pleasure. We have been looking forward to the day we could introduce this to all of you. We love you all so very much also. You know, whatever one does or neglects to do never goes unnoticed in our realm. You are creating, by your work and your diligence, wonderful pearls of Love. Be assured that someday, you will be reaping these pearls. Whatever you create in Love you will reap as well in Love.

We are so grateful here in Telos for this opportunity to be heard and read, and to have a voice on the surface at last. We have been waiting for this type of opportunity for so very long. We have been longing to reconnect "heart-to-heart" with our brothers and sisters on the surface. The bridge between our civilization and your civilization has now been created, though it is stronger on our side than on yours. You must strengthen your bridge with us in a greater way. The heart connections have to be made first from your side with a larger number of people before we can emerge among you visibly. When enough people are ready and willing to accept our teachings, we will make our presence known visually and publicly.

Group - Yes! We can't wait to hear more of your teachings soon. Well again, thank you, beloved friends. It has been absolutely worth hearing your wisdom every second. Until we meet again, blessings to you, Adama, Sananda, Nada and all other members of our Telosian family.

Chapter Seventeen

The Flame of Harmony

A Main Key to Embody to Qualify for Ascension

Final and closing words by Zohar

Aurelia - Zohar is a very ancient master from the city of
Shamballa of the Earth's interior. He tells me that he has
lived 250,000 years in the same body. He measures around
15 feet in height, looks around 35 years of age, and has shining white hair. He adds that his white hair is not due to aging, but the result of the intensity of the white light within
his heart. He is a scientist of nature and of creation, and has
been living in the city of Shamballa most of his life. One of
his favorite subjects is the quality of "harmony" as a main
key to attain the level of consciousness to be admitted into
the Ascension celebration.

*He is also one who over-lighted with his presence, guiding
and assisting the Lemurians in the establishment of the city
of Telos 12,000 years ago when they first moved within the
mountain. He also counseled them in the 5,000 years prior
to that, when Lemuria was destined to be destroyed and they
first began to prepare Telos to be habitable.*

*Zohar tells me that in the beginning, no one in Shamballa
knew what to expect from this Lemurian civilization joining*

the Agartha network inside the Earth. The Council of Light of Shamballa decided then that they needed to be monitored very closely.

Zohar says that after spending much time in Telos in the last 12,000 years, he truly holds a great fondness for that city of Light and Love. What the Lemurians have achieved there in a short time compared to other Earth interior civilizations, surpassed, by far, all the expectations of the planetary and intergalactic councils.

His words are, "I have spent a great deal of time in Telos in the last 12,000 years, especially in the beginning. I have grown to love this place as much as I love my own city of Shamballa. Even now, I spend much time in Telos, but for different reasons. Now I go there, no longer to monitor their progress and their development, but simply because I love and so enjoy being in this wondrous city of Light and in the presence of its inhabitants. The beauty, the abundance, the brotherhood and the creativity that exist in such perfection illustrate better than anywhere else the miracles that Love and Harmony can achieve when a civilization and its people decide, as a collective, to fully embody the Love of the Creator. Telos and her people are an outstanding cosmic example of the wonderment that Love can accomplish."

Zohar also tells me that he has come to the surface a few times in the past and that he enjoyed very much meeting and talking with surface dwellers. He adds, "My heart, as well as the heart of your Lemurian family of Telos, is longing to be able to walk among you again as a brother, and offer my love, my guidance and my wisdom."

Zohar - Greetings, my beloved brothers and sisters, I am Zohar from the city of Shamballa.

Thank you, Aurelia, for asking me to bring my contribution to your book. I am really pleased to offer my energy for such an endeavor, and for the opportunity to connect heart-to-heart with each one of you as you read my message.

Let me say this: In order for this world to be enlightened and to be lifted in the Light, it is necessary that everyone living here take on the persona of "harmony." Everyone must do this; it is a requirement. Otherwise, those who do not will be dragged down by their own arrogance; they will get physically sick from the lack of light and they will die because they will not have the capacity to be happy in the new world. Understand?

This is the choice you now have to make, beloved ones. Either you choose to make it, or you don't. The outcome of your evolution depends entirely on the choices you make each day, and each moment of the day.

The surface populations are getting close to what is called "The Gathering." Know that the powers in this world, the power of the shadow side, the Illuminati and the secret government, are trying to stop this at all costs. However, the more they try to stop it, the more you will know that you are doing it right and that you are coming closer to this great event. Understand?

The governments of your planet do not yet realize that the people who live in the Earth's interior have been there so long, much longer than their limited minds could ever imagine. They do not yet realize that it is not they who are in charge of this planet, and that their time for ruling in separation is soon coming to a dramatic end. Their bubble of illusion will soon be shattered, and they will have to face their cycle of accountability.

It is time now more than ever to distance yourself from those who do not seek to embrace harmony in their lives. All those who wish to embody harmony or wish to be accepted into the family of Telos must do the following:

- You must strive to remain in a state of harmony at all times, with all of creation and all of nature. For without harmony, there is discord and with discord there is destruction.

- Regardless of what people may do or say, "you must remain in harmony." If someone hurts you, bless them and go on with what is your own truth. They do not need to be part of your reality, as it will not serve you.

- If you encounter a disharmonious situation, distance yourself. You have no obligation to remain where harmony does not reign.

- Seek truth and harmony at all times, and do not ever again allow yourself to deviate from this course. Those who continue to resist the new energies now flooding your planet will not be able to persist much longer. These energies are now increasing and doubling each day in order to bring about the changes and transformations you have all been waiting for. Those who resist them will self-destruct.

- You should no longer entertain feelings of discord or guilt. Never be sorry for what you are or what you are going through to balance your debts towards life. Rather strive always to improve yourself and be grateful for the assistance you are receiving.

- Harmony should be the number one quality in your life, and rest assured that it will pave the way for your admittance into the "Halls of Ascension." You will know you have reached that level when nothing bothers you. Whatever people say or do, it will not upset your heart one way or the other.

- Someone who is in total harmony is happy with Creation. That person holds total acceptance of what is. When you become that, you are ready for your ascension.

Since I am almost a Telosian by association, I will also be there to greet you and champion your victory in the Light. Namaste, my beloved friends. I love you all so very much!

A Note about Aurelia Louise Jones

On July 12th, 2009, Aurelia Louise Jones made her transition, leaving us a rich legacy of transformational tools, inspiring us to live from our hearts and fully embrace the Lemurian way of life. Through her channeling of Adama and the Masters of Light, Aurelia's teachings bring forth invaluable "food for thought" which is timeless in its nature. There has never been a more appropriate time than the present moment to attune our hearts to Love, Compassion and above all, Ascension. These are the key elements in Aurelia's heartfelt message from Adama and our Telosian family and all the Ascended Masters of Light and Love. This will set us free, moving us into the next vibrational frequencies, the fifth dimension and beyond.

Aurelia's dream and desire was to awaken humanity during this monumental time of change, to increase the Lemurian Connection around the world and to spread the Light of Adama's message through her books about Telos and the Lemurian way of living. She had great love and a deep gratitude for the planet, beloved Mother Earth, humanity and especially the animals. Her dedication was unwavering and this mission was ever present the last 10 years of her life.

Aurelia's books have touched the lives of thousands of people all over the world. Telos communities have been created in many countries through sheer inspiration to live from the Lemurian Heart. As people embrace the Telos books, study groups are forming to support one another on their sacred spiritual journey. We are grateful to have the Telos books, the teachings and channelings of Aurelia Louise Jones awaken us to our Lemurian heritage.

Mt. Shasta Light Publishing is dedicated to continuing Aurelia's heartfelt mission, spreading the Lemurian teachings and opening our hearts to Ascension. Her work continues to be distributed throughout the world.

Mount Shasta Light Publishing Publications

The Seven Sacred Flames...$39.00

Seven Sacred Flames Prayer Booklet $7.00

Ascension Activation Booklet $7.00

Seven Sacred Flames Card Deck $16.00

Telos Book Series Card Deck $16.00

Telos – Volume 1 "Revelations of the New Lemuria"..$18.00

Telos – Volume 2 "Messages for the Enlightenment
of a Humanity in Transformation"...........................$18.00

Telos – Volume 3 "Protocols of the Fifth Dimension".$20.00

The Effects of Recreational Drugs
on Spiritual Development...$4.00

Angelo's Message – "Angelo, the Angel Cat
Speaks to all People on this Planet Regarding
the Treatment of Animals by Humanity" $8.00

These publications can be purchased in the USA:
- Directly from us by phone or at our mailing address
- From our secure shopping cart on our web site:
http://www.mslpublishing.com
- From Amazon.com
- Bookstores through New Leaf Book Distributing

If ordering by mail, CA residents, please include 8.25% sales tax. Also include shipping charges: Priority or Media mail, according to weight and distance.

Mount Shasta Light Publishing
P.O. Box 1509
Mount Shasta, CA 96067-1509 - USA
aurelia@mslpublishing.com
Phone: (Intl: 001) 530-926-4599
(If no answer, please leave a message)

Telos and Lemurian Connection Associations

Telos USA
www.telos-usa.org
info@telos-usa.org
Also see: Lemurian Connection
www.lemurianconnection.com

Telos World-Wide Foundation, Inc.
E-mail: telos@telosinfo.org
Web Site: www.telosinfo.org

Telos Australia
www.telos-australia.com.au
robert@telos-australia.com.au
catherine@telos-australia.com.au

Telos-France
www.telos-france.com
telosfrance@me.com

Telos Europe
www.teloseurope.eu
telos-europe@me.com

Telos Finland
www.telosfinland.fi
telosfinland@me.com

Telos Japan
www.telos-japan.org
office@telos-japan.org

Canadian Distributors:

Telos World-Wide Foundation, Inc.
7400 St. Laurent, Office 326,
Montreal, QC - H2R 2Y1 – Canada
Phone: (001 Intl.) 1-514-940-7746
E-mail: telos@telosinfo.org
Web Site: www.telosinfo.org

For Canadian Bookstores:
Quanta Books Distributing
3251 Kennedy Road, Unit 20
Toronto, Ontario, MIV-2J0 - CANADA
Phone: 1-888-436-7962 or 416-410-9411
E-mail: quantamail@quanta.ca
Web: www.quanta.ca

**For distributors in other languages
please check our website:
www.mslpublishing.com**